VGM Opportunities Series

OPPORTUNITIES IN ZOOS AND AQUARIUMS

Blythe Camenson

Foreword by
Sydney J. Butler
Executive Director
American Zoo and Aquarium Association

VGM Career Horizons
NTC/Contemporary Publishing Company

JAN - 5 1998

Library of Congress Cataloging-in-Publication Data

Camenson, Blythe.
    Opportunities in zoos and aquariums / Blythe Camenson : foreword
by Sydney J. Butler.
        p.   cm. — (VGM opportunities series)
    ISBN 0-8442-2312-3 (hc). — ISBN 0-8442-2313-1 (pbk.)
    1. Zoos—Vocational guidance.   2. Aquariums—Vocational guidance.
3. Animal specialists—Vocational guidance.   I. Title.   II. Series.
QL76.C35   1997
590'.7'3023—dc21   97-21798
                                                            CIP

Cover Photo Credits:

Cover photographs courtesy of Chicago Zoological Society, by photographers
Jennifer Ocic (top left), Jim Schulz (top right and bottom left), and Mike Greer
(bottom right).

Published by VGM Career Horizons
An imprint of NTC/Contemporary Publishing Company
4255 West Touhy Avenue, Lincolnwood (Chicago), Illinois 60646-1975 U.S.A.
Copyright © 1998 by NTC/Contemporary Publishing Company
Manufactured in the United States of America
International Standard Book Number: 0-8442-2312-3 (hard); 0-8442-2313-1 (soft)
15   14   13   12   11   10   9   8   7   6   5   4   3   2   1

DEDICATION

To longtime friend, Linda Dickinson,
for the special animals we have shared and loved.

CONTENTS

ABOUT THE AUTHOR

A full-time writer of career books, Blythe Camenson's main concern is helping job seekers make educated choices. She firmly believes that with enough information, readers can find long-term, satisfying careers. To that end she researches traditional as well as unusual occupations, talking to a variety of professionals about what their jobs are really like. In all of her books she includes firsthand accounts from people who can reveal what to expect in each occupation.

Blythe Camenson was educated in Boston, earning her B.A. in English and psychology from the University of Massachusetts and her M.Ed. in counseling from Northeastern University.

In addition to *Opportunities in Zoos and Aquariums,* she has written more than two dozen books for NTC/Contemporary Publishing Company.

FOREWORD

In today's world, with so much opportunity in so many professions, why would someone choose to enter and pursue a career in zoos and aquariums? Here are some personal views from someone who, though fascinated with conservation and the environment since childhood, came into this profession only a few years ago.

First, here's some context. Zoos and aquariums are social institutions that have for many centuries brought an unseen natural world to the attention of an eager public. They have changed with the times, but in their own times they have been vastly popular. As far back as 2500 B.C., Egyptians had menageries with oryx, gazelles, baboons, cheetahs, and hyenas. In 150 B.C., Ptolemy VI staged a procession that included 96 elephants drawing chariots, 24 lions, 14 leopards, 14 oryx, 16 cheetahs, and the like. More than 200,000 people jammed into the Paris Exposition in 1900 to view aquatic discoveries and new advances in marine science. And during the summer of 1910, more than a million people streamed into Carl Hagenbeck's Tierpark, near Hamburg, Germany.

Why do I spend time on the past? Because a zoo and aquarium career is the continuation of an ancient and respected tradition that provides an eager and fascinated public with an up-close view of an unseen dynamic living world.

And certainly zoo professionals, though descended from an ancient tradition, are part of a flourishing and vital present. Recreation, exhibitry, education, research, conservation, political influence—these are coins of the realm in today's tremendously important effort to conserve the natural world. And poll after poll will tell you about the public's interest and confidence in zoos and aquariums. Why become involved? Because zoos and aquariums have evolved into important centers for recreation, education, research, and conservation, with public acclaim and necessary influence.

How about the future? How does it look for zoo and aquarium professionals? Here's some more context. First, you will work in a world of tremendous population growth and habitat destruction. Second, you will be functioning in a suspicious and pessimistic country. Most Americans mistrust each other and believe their children's lives will be harder than theirs. With more than 5,000 violent crimes committed each day, you can hardly blame them. That pessimism/worry has led to distrust of government and institutions in general—virtually a nation of suspicious strangers, or, as one newspaper put it, caveman era.

With that background, why would zoos and aquariums survive, much less be good places to spend a career? Here are some personal convictions.

For centuries people have been fascinated with seeing the unseen, natural world up close. And today, where else can people go to have breakfast with dolphins or see orangutans roam free above the crowd? As the urban world closes in, zoos and aquariums open up and celebrate the natural world.

Zoos and aquariums are uniquely equipped to educate and conserve wildlife. No other social institution combines dynamic exhibits, living animals, and a host of professionals dedicated to husbandry, research, rescue/rehabilitation, breeding, and field conservation. This is not calendar conservation, this is everything from test-tube breeding to conserving tigers in Sumatra.

Zoos and aquariums are safe, inexpensive, and fun family places. Before you discount this rather simple notion, name any other social institution that attracts so many *families,* where you see everything—baby strollers, students, volunteers, men and women of all ages. In a world of violent crime, a safe place for families to enjoy themselves is quite an attraction. You can bet that the Walt Disney Corporation is banking on this fact as they prepare to open their new animal park in 1998.

Zoos and aquariums are dynamic; they display and educate about all of the living world. They invite people to look not only at animals, but at the interaction and relationship among all life forms. I believe that the next century will begin an age of biological discovery, moving even beyond the concept of endangered species and habitat protection as we know it. Zoos and aquariums will be great leaders in shaping this discovery, this new vision.

And finally, in a world that's losing its trust and optimism, hope takes on a new importance. It is said that the world belongs to those who bring it the greatest hope, whether it be for a better job, or a better house, or a better environment. And deep down, zoos and aquariums excite the imagination and deliver a powerful message about hope for a better living world.

Listen to Mollie Beattie, former Director of the U.S. Fish and Wildlife Service. "In my lifetime I can remember as a child that zoos were sad sorts of places, places you would go to say goodbye to the moth-eaten remnants of a species. I now know that zoos deeply heighten the enjoyment of all who come, and that, like endangered species, zoos are about understanding and they are about hope."

And listen to George Schaller. "There are never victories in conservation. If you want to save a species or a habitat, it's a fight forevermore... As an ecologist, you walk around the world and see the wounds and scars . . . but then you see the future, and you fight on, with hope. Nothing is ever safe. We have to protect what we still have."

These are eloquent words. They say hope. They say respect. They say keep on going. They should make us proud of our history, our current work. They should give you confidence for the future and some heartfelt answers to the question, "Why a career in zoos and aquariums?"

Sydney J. Butler,
Executive Director
American Zoo and Aquarium Association

ACKNOWLEDGMENTS

The author would like to thank the following professionals for providing information about their careers:

Steven Bailey, Curator of Fishes, New England Aquarium

Shelby Rodney Carter, Assistant Curator/Co-Founder, La Guardar Inc. Wildlife Rehabilitation and Education Center

Scott Dowd, Senior Aquarist, New England Aquarium

Mary Hooper, Volunteer, Phoenix Zoo

Elizabeth Johnson, Senior Zookeeper, Detroit Zoological Institute

Charles LeBlanc, Volunteer, Audubon Zoological Garden, New Orleans

Ron Magill, Zoo Communications Director, Metrozoo, Miami

Christine Miller, Veterinarian, Metrozoo, Miami

Jenny Montague, Assistant Curator/Animal Trainer, New England Aquarium

Karyn Myers, Volunteer, Aquarium of the Americas, New Orleans

Mary Lee Nitschke, Animal Behaviorist/Consultant, Washington Park Zoo

Carin Peterson, Animal Curator, Austin Zoo

Gary Rotter, Commissary Worker, Los Angeles Zoo

Jacky Shaw, Veterinary Technician, Metrozoo, Miami

Heather Urquhart, Senior Aquarist, New England Aquarium

Terry Wolf, Wildlife Director, Lion Country Safari

CHAPTER 1

THE WORLD OF ZOOS
AND AQUARIUMS

More than 120 million people visit zoos and aquariums annually. This huge interest gives dedicated professionals the opportunity to educate the public about the critical need for the conservation of wildlife and wildlands. While this responsibility ensures a varied and rewarding career, the field demands more than a commitment to conservation—it requires hard work.

Although many people might feel otherwise, the truth is that zoo and aquarium work is not always glamorous. It takes a special kind of dedication to care for captive animals. These dependent creatures require attention twenty-four hours a day, seven days a week, on holidays and weekends, and through all sorts of weather.

Most job descriptions for zoo and aquarium work will point out that the requirements for employment include physical strength, the ability to make painstaking observations, and the ability to keep information up-to-date.

Working with exotic animals provides constant challenges, but the rewards for your efforts are great. As a zoo or aquarium professional you are providing the best care for the creatures in your institution. You are also providing opportunities for others to learn how they, too, can participate in the conservation of our planet's natural resources.

ZOOS AND AQUARIUMS

A zoological garden, also known as a zoo, is a facility for keeping wild and domesticated animals available to the public for both education and recreation. There are more than 1,000 zoos in 100 countries, with the largest number present within the United States—approximately 175. These institutions range from small, privately owned collections of limited scope to large public zoos with extensive holdings.

Although most zoos exhibit vertebrate animals, many have aquariums exhibiting marine species. There are approximately 500 public aquariums worldwide, where a large number of different fish and invertebrate species as well as marine reptiles and birds are displayed in huge tanks.

Oceanariums, the newest type of aquarium, often maintain large tanks or holding areas with direct ocean access. These are stocked with some of the largest marine forms, such as dolphins or whales. Visitors observe the animals through glass walls or from overhead walkways.

HOW ZOOS AND AQUARIUMS ORIGINATED

Man first domesticated wild animals during the Stone Age. The first real facilities for keeping these animals captive can be traced back to the twelfth century B.C. in China. There it was common for the ruling classes to keep exotic animals in facilities near their palaces. There were also many zoological collections maintained in the ancient Middle East and Egypt; the most notable were those kept by Queen Hatshepsut and King Solomon of Egypt. In ancient Greece and Rome, collections of captive wild animals were also kept, although most of those were used for competitions. The

Romans captured large African and Indian animals, many of which were used in gladiator sports.

Throughout history some well-known rulers, such as the eighth-century caliph of Baghdad, England's Henry I in the twelfth century, the Mongol emperor Kublai Khan in the thirteenth, and the Aztec's Montezuma II in the sixteenth century, kept zoos and menageries for status and to satisfy their fascination with exotic animals. The Renaissance in Europe marked a new flourishing of private menageries and zoos. During the 1700s several important zoos were built—in Vienna, in Madrid, in Paris—that still exist today. During the transition from monarchies to parliamentary types of government, the existing facilities were either abandoned or converted into public zoos. As a result of the French Revolution, the Jardin des Plantes in Paris became a model for the public zoo we have known in modern times.

The first aquarium opened its doors to the public in 1853 at Regent's Park in England. Where earlier aquariums once maintained numerous small tanks, each with an individual species of freshwater fish, today's facilities may have both freshwater and marine tanks, with capacities of up to one million gallons.

From these early beginnings zoos have gone through an evolution from hubs of entertainment to modern scientific institutions dedicated to education and conservation. With the human population increasing so rapidly since World War II and the destruction of natural habitats for animals that has gone along with it, the need for zoos has become a critical one. Every major zoo in the world has active educational and animal breeding programs. Their main goal is to provide centers for public education. The thrust of that education concerns nature and natural history and the preservation of breeding groups in danger of extinction in their native habitats.

THE CHANGING ROLE OF ZOOS AND AQUARIUMS

For years early modern zoos displayed animals in facilities located in metropolitan areas. Visitors were allowed a close-up view of caged animals that were living in conditions far removed from their native habitat. More recently, zoos have begun participating in the effort to save animal species from extinction and now attempt to simulate homeland conditions in their animal exhibits. These zoological parks have acquired acres and acres of land where animals are allowed to roam more freely during the daytime hours, yet still within a controlled environment that provides protection for the animals and visitors alike. At night, many of the animals are moved from their open territory into smaller holding pens.

In some parks, some species are separated from visitors and other natural enemies within the zoo's collection on islands with moats or walls. Small cages have gone by the wayside for the most part.

Birds are provided with a special lighting system that helps contain them in habitats that have no physical barriers between observers and the birds themselves. Nocturnal animals are also placed in habitats with artificial light-dark cycles. Many of the larger zoos have walk-through or drive-through habitats where birds and other animals can carry on their normal activities.

Some zoos participate in breeding programs for animals that are rare and endangered. Because of the decrease in wild habitats and the resulting reduction in numbers of many species, most zoos rely heavily on captive-bred specimens for display. In the late 1980s about 80 percent of the animals in U.S. zoos were bred in captivity, a big increase over the 25 percent common in the early 1970s.

Today's zoos and aquariums consider the psychological and physical well-being of the animals their highest priority. To achieve this, most facilities have been created to allow animals to participate in as much natural behavior as possible.

BEHIND THE SCENES

Behind the scenes housing, handling, medical, and maternity facilities carry as much weight as the areas open to the public, and often cost more than do the viewing areas.

Most zoos and aquariums are government owned and operated; some are operated by nonprofit societies; and a few are privately owned and commercially operated.

Most governmental zoos depend upon associated support groups for financial aid. The main source for funding for government zoos comes from taxes, although many also receive support from admission charges or from the sale of food or merchandise.

Nonprofit zoos must earn all of their income from admissions, sales, or donations. Privately owned zoos are self-supporting. They often distribute any profits earned above overhead costs to the owners or shareholders.

THE DIFFERENT KINDS OF ZOOS AND AQUARIUMS

Zoos run the gamut, from the traditional city-based facilities that allow visitors close-up views of exhibits, to theme parks spread over several acres and housing a variety of species together. Other open-air exhibits might focus on displaying only one or two species.

Often the facility's name alone will give you an idea of the type of animals displayed. Here is just a small sampling: Parrot Jungle, Monkey Jungle, Lion Country Safari, Sea World, and Butterfly World.

There are many notable zoos and aquariums throughout the world. Some of these are: Taronga Park in Sydney, Australia; Schonbrunn Zoo in Vienna; Antwerp Zoo; Metro Toronto Zoo; Copenhagen Zoo; Tiergarden Park in East Berlin and BERLIN ZOO in West Berlin; the London Zoo; Ueno and Tama zoos in Tokyo; the Amsterdam Zoo; and the Basel and Zurich zoos.

In the United States the following are counted among the top facilities: the New York Zoological Garden (the Bronx Zoo); Philadelphia Zoological Garden; Metrozoo in Miami; San Diego Zoological Garden and the San Diego Wild Animal Park; the Chicago Zoological Park; the Arizona-Sonora Desert Museum in Tucson; the Los Angeles Zoo; Milwaukee Zoological Park; the St. Louis Zoo; and the United States National Zoo in Washington, D.C.

FEATURED FACILITIES

Within this book many job titles are examined and many first-hand accounts are provided by professionals in the field. These professionals work in a variety of settings including:

Aquarium of the Americas, New Orleans
Audubon Zoological Garden, New Orleans
Austin Zoo, Austin, Texas
Detroit Zoological Institute, Royal Oak, Michigan
La Guardar Wildlife Rehabilitation and Education Center,
    Webster, Florida
Lion Country Safari, West Palm Beach, Florida
Los Angeles Zoo, Los Angeles
Metrozoo, Miami
New England Aquarium, Boston
Phoenix Zoo, Phoenix
Washington Park Zoo, Portland, Oregon

JOBS WITHIN ZOOS AND AQUARIUMS

Most public facilities for the display of animals are run similar to the way small cities operate. Most employees of zoos and aquariums are concerned with administration, office procedures, or maintenance of grounds and facilities.

As within a city, though, the positions that are most vital relate closely to the care and well-being of its "citizens." These positions include curators, keepers, and veterinarians.

Professional job classifications within zoos and aquariums can fall into several categories including administration, collections, conservation, curation, education, development (fund-raising), exhibit design, husbandry, public relations, marketing, research, veterinary services, visitor services, and volunteer services.

In addition zoos and aquariums employ a large team of support staff including security guards, maintenance workers, grounds-keepers, landscape architects, and secretarial and other office workers. Further, zoos and aquariums depend heavily upon volunteers and student interns to round out the professional staff. (More information about volunteering is in Chapter 9.)

Although not every job title is found in all facilities, many are common to each kind of zoo. The job description, however, will vary depending on the institution. Curators and veterinarians, for example, are found in almost every kind of zoo or aquarium, even though the collections they deal with and their specific duties are very different. Aquarists, on the other hand, are usually found only in aquariums, where their specialized skills are most needed.

Depending upon the institution, some job titles whose duties are the same will carry different designations. For example, curators may be called coordinators or wildlife or conservation directors; zookeepers may be called animal caretakers, animal keepers, or aquarists.

The American Zoo and Aquarium Association (AZA) has identified dozens of both direct and zoo-related career categories. Below is an alphabetical list of the job titles found within broad categories (departments and department names and responsibilities will vary from institution to institution) with a brief description for each. In this book only those job titles directly related to animal care, collection, and education and exhibition will be covered. Jobs such as operations or gift shop can be found in a variety of settings other than zoos and aquariums. Information on these non-zoo-related careers can be found in the *Occupational Outlook Handbook* or in other NTC/VGM Career Horizon books.

JOB TITLES

Administration

Assistant Director. The assistant director works closely with the director and assumes responsibility in the director's absence.

Director/Chief Operating Officer. The director carries out policies that are dictated by the facility's governing authority. He or she is responsible for the institution's operation and plans for future development.

Finance Manager/Director. The finance manager oversees the institution's finances, including accounts payable, purchasing, investments, and the preparation of financial statements.

Operations Director/Manager. The operations manager is responsible for the daily operation of the institution's physical plant and equipment.

Personnel Manager/Director. The personnel manager is responsible for all personnel matters including payroll, insurance, and tax matters.

Registrar. The registrar maintains computer records on the animal collection and applies for permits and licenses to hold or transport animals.

Conservation

Conservation Biologist/Zoologist. These scientists provide scientific and technical assistance in the management of the animal collection and assist in conducting various research or field conservation projects.

Curator/Coordinator/Director of Conservation. These professionals oversee an institution's conservation activities, including field projects. They also serve as liaisons with government wildlife agencies and other conservation organizations.

Curatorial

Curator of Animals. Animal curators manage a certain section of an institution's collection, for example, mammals, birds, fish, or reptiles.

Curator of Exhibits. Exhibits curators design, create, and build exhibits and assist in the design of graphics.

Curator of Horticulture. These horticulture experts are responsible for the botanical collection and its application to the animal collection. They may supervise aquarists in the daily maintenance of aquarium plant life or be responsible for the maintenance of the institution's grounds.

General Curator. The chief curator oversees an institution's entire animal collection and animal management staff. He or she is responsible for strategic collection planning.

Head Keeper/Aquarist. Supervisory keepers or aquarists oversee a section or department of the institution; they provide training and scheduling for keepers.

Junior Keeper. Some institutions offer a summer program for high school students who choose to volunteer in a zoo or aquarium. Duties are similar to those of older volunteers, but junior keepers are supervised much more closely.

Keeper/Aquarist. The aquarist provides daily care to the institution's animals, including diet preparation, cleaning, general exhibit maintenance, and record keeping. Some aquarists also participate in research and collections activities.

Senior Keeper/Aquarist. These advanced keepers and aquarists provide primary animal care for a department.

Trainer. Animal trainers work with wildlife to make them more comfortable being handled by humans, specifically veterinarian staff and caretakers. Training also can include encouraging the natural behavior of the animal for educational purposes.

Development

Development Director/Officer. Development professionals develop and manage an institution's fund-raising activities, which can include writing grant proposals and attracting corporate sponsors, in addition to searching out private donations.

Membership Director/Manager. Membership directors are responsible for maintaining and increasing institution memberships for families and individuals and designing special events for members only. They may also be in charge of "adopt-an-animal" programs.

Education

Curator of Education/Education Director. Professionals within a zoo's or aquarium's education department plan and implement the institution's education programs and act as a liaison between the facility and the press and general public.

Public Relations and Marketing

Marketing Director/Manager. Marketing personnel create advertising campaigns and organize other activities to increase public awareness of the institution.

Public Relations/Affairs Manager/Director. PR professionals promote the institution, its mission, and its programs to the public via the media.

Special Events Manager/Coordinator. These professionals develop and implement events and activities to attract visitors to the institution throughout the year.

Research

Curator/Coordinator/Director of Research. Head researchers supervise research projects, serve as liaison between the institution and the academic community, and publish articles in scientific journals. They also work closely with the conservation and curatorial staff.

Veterinarian Services

Veterinarian. Veterinarians are responsible for the health-care program for the animal collection and the maintenance of health records.

Veterinary Technician. Vet techs assist the veterinarian and provide care to the animals under the supervision of the veterinarian.

Visitor Services

Gift Shop Manager. The gift shop manager supervises staff and all aspects of gift shop operation from buying merchandise to designing the shops.

Visitor Services Manager. The director or manager of the visitor services department supervises the staff and facilities that cater to the visiting public including concessions and rest rooms.

Volunteer Services

Docent/Tour Guide/Volunteer. Duties for these nonpaid staff members vary and can include diet preparation, small animal care, teaching educational programs, leading group tours, and staffing special events.

Volunteer Coordinator. The volunteer coordinator usually has a paid position and is responsible for recruiting and maintaining a staff of volunteers and docents (tour guides). Duties include scheduling docents for on- and off-grounds activities and keeping docents abreast of new developments to relate to the public.

CHOOSING A CAREER

With so many different kinds of zoos and aquariums and the varied job categories they support, how do you know which avenue would be right for you? Take a look at the chart below. Find your interests and skills, then look across to identify career options. You'll see that many of the job titles combine more than one interest.

Interests and Skills	Job Titles
Working with animals	aquarist, curator, trainer, veterinarian, veterinarian technician, zookeeper
Working with your hands	aquarist, curator, exhibit builder, exhibit designer, trainer, veterinarian, veterinarian technician, zookeeper
Finding out information	aquarist, curator, researcher, scientist

Interests and Skills	*Job Titles*
Working with the public	curator, educator, information officer, marketing, public relations, security, special activities coordinator, tour guide
Working outdoors	aquarist, curator, tour guide, trainer, zookeeper

THE QUALIFICATIONS YOU'LL NEED

Required qualifications vary depending on the job. Although many employers prefer their applicants to have a bachelor's or higher degree in any number of fields, not all do. In some situations the following qualifications are more important: prior experience working with animals in zoos or similar settings, the ability to communicate with diverse groups of people, and good writing and research skills.

More and more these days, however, prior experience *and* a four-year degree are what employees seek—and because of the keen interest and competition for zoo and aquarium jobs, they have no trouble finding people with the right combination of qualifications.

The conservation and scientific programs in zoos and aquariums have become highly technical and specialized. Employers look for formal training in animal science, zoology, marine biology, conservation biology, wildlife management, and animal behavior. Typically, advanced degrees are required for curatorial, research, and conservation positions. But advanced academic credentials alone are often considered insufficient, and it may take many years of on-the-job training for someone to learn the hands-on practical aspects of exotic animal care. A few zoos and aquariums offer curatorial internships that are designed to provide practical experience.

When choosing an academic program for animal-related careers, it is a good idea to review the curriculum of the particular schools you are considering because some programs focus more on zoological applications than others.

For those interested in the business side of zoo and aquarium operations, courses should include those areas and skills related to the particular area of expertise, such as accounting, public relations, marketing, or personnel management.

For some job titles, additional training or qualifications are necessary. For example, all aquarists must be certified divers and veterinarians, and vet techs must have specialized training in their particular disciplines.

THE JOB HUNT

Although many animal lovers can find employment in their own hometown, in order to broaden your opportunities, chances are you'll have to relocate. If you have a spot in mind where you'd like to work, a phone call or an introductory letter sent with your resume is a good way to start. If you would like some more ideas on possible locations, there are several professional associations and zoo directories listed in Appendix A that can lead you to interesting destinations. These professional associations produce monthly or quarterly newsletters with job listings and upcoming internships and fellowships.

Ask any zoo or aquarium professional the best way to get your foot in the door and they will tell you that being on-site and hearing about openings firsthand is the way to go. How can you be in the right place at the right time? Volunteer. Opportunities for volunteer positions are covered in Chapter 9.

Many professionals who have worked their way up the ladder to positions with varying levels of responsibility started as a volunteer or student intern. When an entry-level position opened up, they jumped at the chance to prove themselves. Hard work, enthusiasm, and dedication will not go unnoticed.

SALARIES

Salaries vary widely from position to position, but are generally low, as are most pay scales for education-related fields. Factors such as the source of funding or the region of the country determine salary levels more so than the complexity of the job or the level of the candidates' education and experience. Institutions located in metropolitan areas generally offer higher salaries than those located in smaller cities or towns.

Some jobs pay only hourly wages, others follow the federal government's GS scale. A tour guide might volunteer his or her time or earn $6 to $10 an hour. An animal keeper's salary can range from minimum wage to more than $30,000 a year, depending on skills and the amount of time put in at a particular institution. An assistant curator could earn from $25,000 to $30,000 a year, a trainer or veterinarian in a zoo setting from $30,000 to $40,000 or more.

Most jobs provide benefits such as health insurance. But all those interviewed on the pages to come stressed that financial rewards were not the main reason—or even a consideration—in pursuing their chosen professions. The low pay is far outweighed by the satisfaction of doing work they love.

THE EMPLOYMENT OUTLOOK

For every opening, personnel staff report receiving hundreds of applications from qualified and eager applicants. Zoo and aquarium work is very attractive to many people, thus causing keen competition for all job seekers.

The job outlook is also negatively affected by expected slow growth in zoo capacity and low turnover.

However, this does not mean that the situation is hopeless. In the pages to come you will learn how other zoo and aquarium professionals got started, and through their firsthand expert advice you will find a few strategies on how you, too, can get your foot in the door.

CHAPTER 2

ZOOKEEPERS

All zoos and aquariums employ keepers, the personnel directly responsible for the care of the animals and their enclosures. Job titles and duties vary by employment setting, but there are several responsibilities all keepers have in common. Keepers prepare the diets, clean the enclosures, and monitor the behavior of exotic animals. They feed, water, groom, bathe, and exercise animals. Sometimes they also play with the animals or provide companionship, and they observe behavioral changes that could indicate illness or injury.

Keepers might also help in the designing, building, and repairing of enclosures or cages. They might also care for the plants in and around the exhibits.

Keepers sometimes assist in research studies. Depending upon the species, the keepers may also train the animals. An example is the elephant keeper who teaches the pachyderm to hold up its foot so that the veterinarian may examine the sole.

In addition, keepers may put on shows and give lectures to the public.

Zookeepers who work in aquariums usually are called *aquarists*. This interesting career and its setting is covered in depth in Chapter 7.

WORKING CONDITIONS

People who love animals get satisfaction from working with and helping animals. However, some of the work may be physically demanding and unpleasant. Zookeepers have to clean animal cages and lift heavy supplies like bales of hay. Also, the work setting is often noisy. Some duties, such as euthanizing a hopelessly injured or aged animal, may be emotionally stressful.

Zookeepers can be exposed to bites, kicks, and diseases from the animals they attend. Keepers may work outdoors in all kinds of weather. Hours are irregular. Animals have to be fed every day, so caretakers rotate weekend shifts. In some zoo animal hospitals, an attendant is on duty twenty-four hours a day, which means night shifts. Most full-time zookeepers work about forty hours a week, some work fifty hours a week, or more.

In spite of the odd hours and hard work, zookeeping jobs are at a premium. Although competition is fierce, the job outlook is good as opportunities continue to expand.

TRAINING FOR ZOOKEEPERS

The educational requirements for entry-level zookeeping jobs vary, but most zoological parks require their keepers to have a bachelor's degree in biology, animal science, zoology, or a related field. With so much competition for jobs these days, zoos have the luxury of choosing the most qualified applicants. Employers might also require experience with animals, preferably as a volunteer in a zoo or as a paid keeper in a smaller zoo. Other experience that is helpful includes work with animals in diverse settings such as shelters, pet grooming salons, veterinarian offices, or hospitals. Certainly the more educational credentials you have, coupled with hands-on experience, will enhance your employment chances.

Some colleges have specific programs oriented toward zoo careers. One such program is offered by the Santa Fe Community College's Teaching Zoo in Gainesville, Florida. Another is the Exotic Animal Training Management Program that Moorepark College in California offers. The American Association of Zookeepers, whose address is listed in Appendix A, is a good source for training and education information for potential zookeepers.

But education and experience are not all that it takes. Successful zookeepers should be knowledgeable about the animals in their facilities as well as the animals' natural habitat and behavior.

Zookeepers also often interact with the public. They need to be friendly, outgoing, and professional and be able to answer questions from visitors.

Zookeeping is demanding work requiring physical strength, commitment, and dedication. Employers look for reliable people who are willing to learn and take their work seriously. The lives and well-being of the animals depend upon the care of the zookeeper. This role is an extremely important one.

Once hired, most facilities provide on-the-job training, and most zookeepers start off in a zookeeper-in-training capacity before moving into a full zookeeper job title.

ADVANCEMENT

Most zoos have career ladders for zookeepers. They might start out as zookeepers-in-training, then move from junior zookeeper to full zookeeper, then up to senior zookeeper and even supervisor. Some, after many years of experience, can move into curatorial and administrative positions. But as is true with most job settings, the higher up you go, the less hands-on work you encounter. Many zookeepers who prefer direct contact with the animals will halt

their own advancement so as not to get bogged down in the paperwork that accompanies more administrative work.

ZOOKEEPER RANKINGS

Here is an example of the keeper rankings found at Lion Country Safari in West Palm Beach, Florida. (You will find more information on Lion Country Safari in Chapter 3.)

Keeper 1. An entry-level position requiring a bachelor's degree in
a life science or at least two years' experience at a zoological facility.

Keeper 2. This rank demands the same requirements as the
Keeper 1 position except that another year or two of experience is
expected.

Keeper 3. This rank would go to someone with a bachelor's
degree and at least five years experience.

Keeper 4. This position requires at least a bachelor's degree and
between seven and nine years experience.

To start at any of the higher ranks, a zookeeper would be trans-
ferring from another facility or working his or her way up the
ranks at the original facility.

SALARIES FOR ZOOKEEPERS

Salaries in zoo professions are not glamorous and can vary a
great deal depending on the region of the country in which the
facility is located and the source of funding. However, most entry-
level zookeepers with a bachelor's degree start somewhere in the
high teens to low twenties and work their way up the salary scale
over time.

As an example, at Lion Country Safari the Keeper 1 position pays about $7.00 an hour and goes up to $7.50 or more for the next rank. The Keeper 4 position would pay about $24,000.

CLOSE-UP: DETROIT ZOOLOGICAL INSTITUTE

The Detroit Zoological Institute comprises three facilities: the Detroit Zoo with 125 acres of naturalistic habitat in Royal Oak, approximately ten miles north of Detroit; and the Belle Isle Zoo and Belle Isle Aquarium, both located on Belle Isle, an island park in Detroit.

The Detroit Zoological Institute features a total collection of 2,500 to 3,000 animals. At the Detroit Zoo approximately 1,200 to 1,300 animals are exhibited. This includes mammals, birds, reptiles, amphibians, and invertebrates of some 250 species.

The Belle Isle Zoo has about 200 animals of 40 to 50 species, and the Belle Isle Aquarium typically exhibits about 1,500 animals made up of mostly fish with some reptiles, amphibians, and invertebrates.

The Detroit Zoological Institute strives to promote respect, appreciation, and ethical attitudes toward wildlife and works toward conservation programs for the survival of endangered species.

Volunteering at the Detroit Zoological Institute

An important function of the Education Division is the Detroit Zoo Docent Association. This is a group of well-trained volunteers who act as informed guides for groups visiting the zoo, transforming the experience from a simple visit to education about wildlife.

Volunteers are an important part of the Detroit Zoological Institute, and they offer volunteer opportunities for people of all ages.

Gallery Guides are the volunteer staff of the Wildlife Interpretive Gallery. Training is given in a short four-hour period. Guides help visitors as they enjoy the coral reef aquarium, butterfly and hummingbird garden, film theater, permanent art collection, and changing exhibit hall. No prior experience is required, and training includes an information manual and the opportunity to learn about butterflies and coral reefs.

Docents are volunteer educators. Docents participate in a longer training program of ten weeks and learn all about the Zoological Institute and the animal collection. Docents lead group tours, teach outreach programs for schools and community groups, narrate tractor-train tours, and work on special projects with the curatorial staff.

Adopt-a-Gardeners take care of the dozens of gardens around the Detroit Zoological Park. This is a chance for avid amateur gardeners to show off their gardening skills to more than one million visitors per year.

For more information about volunteering at the Detroit Zoological Institute, contact the education division. To learn about volunteering in general, turn to Chapter 9.

FIRSTHAND ACCOUNTS
Elizabeth Johnson, Senior Zookeeper

Elizabeth Johnson is a senior zookeeper at the Detroit Zoological Institute in Royal Oak, Michigan. She earned her B.S. in biology in 1988 from Saginaw Valley State University in Saginaw, Michigan, and her M.S. in biology in 1995 from Wayne State University Graduate School in Detroit. Elizabeth has been working in the field since 1988.

GETTING STARTED

"Actually zookeeping never occurred to me as a career. I was going to school for a career in research involving animals. After graduating from Saginaw Valley State University in May 1988, I was hired by the Belle Isle Nature Center. I was responsible for performing naturalist duties, such as caring for the animals in their shelter, giving talks, and doing rehabilitation work with injured wildlife.

"In March of 1989, while still employed with the nature center, I was picking up an application for another job when I found out that the city had just opened the position for zookeeper and was accepting applications. I decided to turn in an application; I was hired by the Detroit Zoo three months later."

WHAT THE JOB IS LIKE

"I have been employed at the Detroit Zoological Institute for almost eight years now. Zookeeping is a very interesting career. It seems as though there are never two days alike. You learn something new every day. When I first started, I could not believe I was actually getting paid for doing what I was doing.

"I have been taking care of elephants and rhinos for seven and a half years now. Recently, our elephant unit has picked up the care of the giraffe, too. There are five keepers in the elephant unit. We have three female Asian elephants (ages 32, 39, and 46), one black rhino (age 45), and three giraffes (two males ages 5 and 15, and one female age 11). A typical day for me begins with all the keepers meeting in the administration basement so that the head keepers can pass out daily duties or advise us on any changes that have taken place. The keepers then all go to the exhibit they are assigned to for that day. For me, I start either at the elephant house or the giraffe house (taking turns among the keepers in our unit).

"The first order of business is to check all the animals under your care that day to make sure all are well. Then the fun part begins—all the cleaning of the exhibits! The cleaning usually takes a couple of hours. Then every day at 10:30 we bathe our elephants for the public to see. The bath usually lasts for about an hour. During the bath we hose them off, scrub their skin to remove any stains, and perform foot care on them. Since elephants in captivity are restricted to the area in their exhibit, foot care is very important. We file and sand their nails to prevent them from growing too long. If their nails are too long, they can become cracked and lead to further problems. We also trim their cuticles regularly, and most important, we trim the bottom of their feet. The bottom of an elephant's foot is like a hard callous that can get many cracks and grooves. If these cracks and grooves are not cleaned out and trimmed, they can lead to infection. We do a little foot care on each elephant daily. We keep the sessions short and pleasant. The elephants don't seem to mind at all, they are used to their routine foot care. During the bath we scrub their skin so as not to get a build up of dead skin. After the bath, if it is during the summer, we will lead them into the pool in their yard. After coming out of their pool they will head directly to their sandbox and start dusting themselves to protect their skin from the sun and insects. If it is too cold, they will get sawdust for dusting.

"Usually by now it is lunchtime. After lunch, at 1:00, we perform a demonstration with the elephants for the public. We will tail them up and walk them around the pool and then work them individually with each picking up logs, pushing logs, and lying down. After the demonstration we give each elephant a treat bucket of hay and then answer any questions from the public.

"During the winter we have the elephants do laps inside for exercise. After this we usually go "browse hunting" for our animals. We venture out for grapevine, mulberry, elm, maple, sorghum, and bamboo. Of course, browse hunting is limited in the winter here in Michigan, but the elephants still eat trees with no leaves. Occasionally, they will also get palm that has been trimmed back from the birdhouse.

"The few hours left in the day we spend providing behavioral enrichment for our animals and doing extra cleaning of our exhibits and extra duty handed out from the head keepers. This can include unloading hay-truck pellets, moving other animals to different exhibits, cutting grass, whacking weeds, cleaning exhibit pools, performing overall maintenance of our buildings (painting, dusting), and just helping out other keepers on their exhibits doing jobs too labor intensive for one person.

At this point in the day it is time to start closing up the exhibits. The animals' food is put down and the animals are brought inside and secured for the evening. A little more cleaning and the day is over.

"The job can be either busy or relaxed. It just depends on the day. Overall, I feel by keeping busy during the day, you go home feeling as if you have accomplished quite a bit. You feel more rewarded."

THE UPSIDES AND DOWNSIDES

"Working with elephants can be very rewarding. In a sense you are more than just a handler, you are actually part of their herd, your little family away from home. Elephants are very intelligent and affectionate animals and a pleasure to work with. I have learned quite a lot. You have respect for them and they respect you. It's a mutual relationship. Knowing that you are responsible for the daily care of these animals and doing it correctly and efficiently leaves you with a great feeling. Observing your animals also can be fun—watching them eat the trees you just cut down for them or watching the elephants splash and play in the big sprinkler you hooked up over their sandbox. Just knowing that you are doing your utmost to make sure that these animals have the best possible care that you can give them is very rewarding.

"You can also be rewarded in other ways. I have been sent to three elephant managers' conferences. At one I presented a paper I wrote with one of my co-workers.

"It's never boring, but you can get cabin fever in the winter. The animals, too. But I really don't dislike that so much as I do some of the politics that can get in the way, such as disagreeing with your boss."

A WORD OF ADVICE

"You should realize that taking care of animals is a great responsibility and you need to do the best you possibly can. Being a zookeeper can be a very rewarding and educational career."

Gary Rotter, Commissary Worker

Although Gary Rotter's current job does not involve direct contact with the animals, he is involved in work that is crucial to their well-being. He works in the Los Angeles Zoo's commissary, which is responsible for all supplies, particularly the food, needed for animal care. This is how Gary got started:

"Working in the commissary is a foot in the door for me toward a career in animal keeping. There are several current keepers who started in the commissary, and I plan on following in their footsteps. My goal is to be picked up as an animal keeper when they hire keepers again. By combining my job performance and the training I received from the keeper class, I hope that this will be my path toward animal keeping.

"The animals I want to work with the most are the chimps. Their behavior fascinates me.

"My education is as follows: I graduated high school in 1990; attended one semester of junior college in 1991, majoring in administration of justice; and then I started correspondence school in 1992 as an animal care technician. I ultimately completed the animal keeper class at Los Angeles Community College in 1996.

"I started my current job in January of 1995. My love for animals and the environment inspired me to seek a career in the zoo business. Having many pets at home, I was able to observe and enjoy their behavior, and it fascinated me.

"At the time, I didn't know the correct path to a career in the zoo world, but I was fortunate enough to read in the local newspaper about volunteers needed for the zoo's behavioral enrichment group. This is a group of people who work to make the animals' time more enjoyable by renovating exhibits and setting up toys or food treats for the animals. Unfortunately, I did not have the time to volunteer then—but my brother did.

"With similar interests and a superior work ethic, my brother quickly built himself a terrific reputation. Within months, a job opened at the zoo commissary, and he was approached about employment. He accepted and impressed everyone with his efficiency and accuracy and hunger for more. Then, fortunately for me, another job opened in the commissary. Needless to say, as the brother of this work maniac, I was hired in hopes of being a good duplicate.

"My work will vary on a day-by-day basis. I fill animal diet orders for each exhibit. I follow the diets created by the curators and vets. The diets consist of produce and meat and fish. I deliver those orders as well as hay and grain to the exhibits. I also cut and deliver browse (tree branches with edible leaves) and maintain the cleanliness of our work areas, including the hay dock and grain storage area.

"My days are spent both indoors and out. The workload varies depending on the day and the time. Close visual contact with the animals is all I get in this particular position. My hours are from 7:00 A.M. to 3:30 P.M.

"What I like the most about my job is that I get a variety of things to do each day. What I like least is the fact I have to work my five days a week, even on holidays. But the animals need to eat, so I have to work.

"My advice for any prospective commissary or zoo employee is to have a strong back. You'd better not mind getting dirty, too. And do not think you are going to get rich. Most of all make sure you like animals."

CHAPTER 3

ZOO CURATORS

The curation department in most zoos is responsible for the acquisition of animals whether through breeding, trading with other institutions, or collecting from the wild. Equally important curatorial functions include the establishment of standards of animal care and housing and the supervision of animal-care personnel.

The general curator or director oversees the entire operation, with many zoos divided into specific departments, each with their own curator or department head.

THE CURATOR'S ROLE

Animal Acquisition

Almost all new zoo acquisitions are developed through breeding programs, either at the particular zoo or through other zoos with active breeding programs. Some animals are acquired from governmental agencies involved in conservation. Only a small percentage these days come directly from the wild.

If a zoo has a surplus of one particular species, these animals might be traded from one zoo to another.

Government bodies, both local and international, strictly control the acquisition of zoo animals. All animals crossing state lines or coming from other countries must have documentation showing that the various laws and regulations have not been violated at either the point of origin or the destination. In addition various government agencies rigorously inspect animal housing, transportation, and care.

Curators often act as a liaison with the various government agencies to ensure that all regulations are followed and that animals are transported with the utmost care.

Some curators are also involved with breeding activities for their particular zoo. The International Species Inventory System (ISIS) is a computerized registry providing detailed information about the holdings in more than 200 zoos throughout the world. Zoo curators consult these data to help develop sound programs for breeding animals in captivity.

Supervisory and Administrative Work

Most curators will tell you that the farther up the ladder they go, the less hands-on interaction they have with the animals. For those zoo professionals who enter the field because of their love for animals, this is a downside. However, while curators might not be involved with the day-to-day care of their charges, they are still involved, making sure that care is provided to the highest standard. This involvement is carried out through supervising a staff of animal caretakers and senior zookeepers.

To do this effectively, curators, in addition to their many skills working with animals, must have good people skills and communication skills.

To handle all their administrative responsibilities, curators must also be computer literate and be able to pay attention to the details of all the required documentation.

SPECIALIZATIONS

In addition to general administrative duties, most curators are placed in specialized departments in charge of, for example, reptiles or large animals, the aviary, or the zoo nursery.

Some curators work with horticulture and are responsible for the physical landscaping of the facilities; others are mainly involved in conservation projects, the rescue and rehabilitation of stranded animals, or research.

Generally speaking, successfully running a zoo depends on strong teamwork, and curators and other staff learn to work closely with colleagues in their own and other departments.

TRAINING AND ADVANCEMENT

Many curators start off as zookeepers and work their way up the ranks. It would be extremely rare for a new college graduate to walk directly into a curation position. These days, the minimum requirement for a zookeeper is a bachelor's degree in a field related to zoo work. In addition to this, hands-on experience is usually required. (See Chapter 2 for more information.) Future curators often begin work as zookeepers and after many years of experience earned on the job and with demonstrated leadership qualities, they may move into supervisory or more administrative positions.

Because the number of qualified applicants for zookeeper positions far exceeds the number of openings, competition is keen. Those with their eyes on a future curator's job need to prepare themselves in every aspect of zoo-animal care and be prepared to start with cleaning cages or preparing meals.

Because zoos vary in size and the opportunities available, advancement might depend on relocating from one zoo to another.

Working in the field and staying in touch with colleagues through professional associations and conferences is the main way people learn about new curatorial job openings.

SALARIES FOR CURATORS

Zookeepers often begin at the bottom of the salary scale, usually in the high teens or low twenties. As they move up the ranks to positions of increasing responsibility, their salaries move up, too. Curators earn anywhere between $30,000 to $55,000 or $60,000, depending upon the facility's budget and the amount of experience and seniority curators have amassed.

CLOSE-UP: LION COUNTRY SAFARI

Lion Country Safari, a private zoological park in West Palm Beach, Florida, offers visitors the chance to drive through 500 acres of natural wildlife preserve. More than 1,000 wild animals from all over the world roam freely including lions, giraffes, chimpanzees, bison, ostrich, antelope, elephants, rhinos, and many more. On the grounds there is also a petting zoo, a newborn nursery, paddleboats, and a campground.

Lion Country Safari's philosophy is to educate and entertain as well as provide a safe habitat where many endangered species may live and breed.

The Curator's Role at Lion Country Safari

There are two curators at Lion Country Safari, each responsible for different areas of the park as well as for the people who take care of those areas:

The Curator of the Preserve is responsible for the drive-through area of the park. This person manages the care of all the large antelope, lions, elephants, chimps, and others; organizes and schedules the keepers and makes sure that everything that is supposed to be accomplished in a day gets done; and works closely with the director (see the firsthand account of Lion Country Safari's wildlife director below) suggesting breeding plans and programs.

The Curator of the Nursery manages this area in the walk-through section of the park. The curator is responsible for the nursery itself and also for the bird and primate exhibits, the reptile park, the petting zoo, and the hospital.

Curators at Lion Country Safari earn about $30,000 a year.

FIRSTHAND ACCOUNTS

Terry Wolf, Wildlife Director, Lion Country Safari

Terry Wolf is the wildlife director at Lion Country Safari. He is responsible for all animal-oriented operations in the park including husbandry, diet, construction of exhibits, breeding programs, personnel training, and acquisitions of materials and feed. He supervises twenty-five keepers, two curators, and an animal manager.

TERRY WOLF'S BACKGROUND

"I have always had a love for animals. When I was a kid I worked in poodle shops and pet shops. One of the first jobs I had was bathing dogs and taking care of them. I guess I could blame my mother for this. She got me involved in a lot of this when I was younger, especially working with dogs.

"I had a break in college and needed to find work, so I applied at Lion Country Safari and got a job in the maintenance department.

That was in 1970. I worked my way up the ranks through the entertainment end of it, taking care of the boat ride and other rides. But I always wanted to be a keeper, and, when an opening came about, I applied and was hired. I worked up through the ranks on that side and I was transferred to another park in Texas, owned by the same people, where I was made a manager. I stayed there for several years, but they went bankrupt in the seventies, so I went back to school and got my master's degree.

"I then came back to Lion Country Safari in the early eighties, and because there were no upper-level jobs open at the time, I took a temporary position working the elephant ride (which no longer exists). But within six months I was promoted to the wildlife director position."

WORKING AT LION COUNTRY SAFARI

"I enjoy working with the animals the most, but now a lot of my job involves people and management and safety concerns. I still have to work hard to keep my touch with the animals and to work with them. Most of us prefer to work with the animals, and we just put up with the other stuff.

"Right now, in addition to my other duties, I am directly responsible for the training of elephant keepers and chimp keepers. I am the only experienced person here in those two fields. I enjoy the chimps and the elephants the most. I work closely with them and find them to be some of the most intelligent animals on earth. The elephants have real personalities—they are real characters. And they live for such a long time.

"We are working on a new lion exhibit, too. The lions are kept in a building at night—it's the state law—but they stay out during the day. A keeper patrols the vicinity—we have zebra-striped trucks for him or her to ride around in—not only to keep an eye on the lions, but to make sure that people don't get out of their cars. The lions appear to be tame, but they are not. They behave here just as they would in the wild, letting cars come up close to them. If you were to get out of the car, though, they would feel intimidated and might attack.

"We work with the animals every day. Besides the lions, the elephants are moved into a barn at night and the giraffes and antelope go into holding pens. We have conditioned them to respond when we call them, to round them up so we can get a head count and check on them. We try to make them as comfortable as possible working with us.

"Any time you deal with life, you deal with death, and that's the downside to my work. Sometimes we lose an animal that we've known for a long time. You get pretty close to them and it's hard. Just recently we had to euthanize an old chimp I'd known since I started working in the park in 1970. He was about 55 years old and had severe arthritis in his spine. The pain was just tearing him down. It's tough to deal with."

A WORD OF ADVICE

"You need to stay in school. Education is becoming more and more important. The market is limited, there are limited keeper jobs available, and there is a lot of competition. All around the country the educational standards are being raised every year. Within ten years a master's degree will be needed to get anywhere. And to get into management, it's almost mandatory that you have a master's degree.

"Experience is always helpful, but it's harder now to get the experience without the education. There are places you can volunteer, such as wildlife conservation organizations, or you can get experience in other settings such as farms and ranches or veterinarian clinics. Those all help toward building your resume and at least getting an interview. Whenever we have an opening for an entry-level position—and Lion Country Safari, compared to a lot of other places, has a pretty small budget—we still get thirty or forty applications from around the country."

Carin Peterson, Animal Curator, Austin Zoo, Texas

Carin Peterson earned her B.A. in zoology in 1991 and is currently working on a master's degree in wildlife biology. She has attended seminars and has participated in veterinary technician training. She started working in the field in 1992.

"I have always been interested in research science and nature and especially animals, and I thought this would be a good way to combine all my interests. Basically, I saw an ad in the local newspaper looking for an animal caretaker. I came to the zoo for an interview and was hired on the spot. I started out as a zookeeper and worked my way up to the animal department supervisor. We are a small zoo, so the chances for advancement here probably happen quicker than they do at a larger institution.

"My job duties vary from day-to-day, although there are some things that always have to be done. My basic job description includes the following: maintaining the animal records, coordinating veterinary care and visits, advising on diets and husbandry, providing input on acquisitions and departures (sometimes coordinating them), and supervising and training the keeper staff.

"I also do the following: answer our e-mail, maintain our webpage, work with some basic animal training, and fill in for keeper staff when someone is absent.

"The animal training can be as complicated as teaching an animal an extensive series of behaviors ("tricks") or as simple as getting an animal to accept human presence without stress. In reality, however, this may not be that simple and may take as long to teach as training another animal to do a complicated behavior. We mostly train animals to be used in educational programs. This means getting them acclimated to a leash or harness or accepting human contact such as being handled and picked up without stress.

"The method of training we use is called operant conditioning (also known as bridge-target training), which uses positive reinforcement to shape desired behaviors. There are many people who have extensive experience with this type of training, both in the domestic and exotic animal worlds. We had seminars taught by these specialists in-house. The American Zoo and Aquarium Association (AZA) and the American Association of Zookeepers (AAZK) can provide more information. [See Appendix A.]

"Usually my day is pretty relaxed, but that can change in an instant. There can be a lot of stress involved, especially if there is a complicated veterinary procedure to be done or an animal is sick or pregnant, if the weather is bad, or if there are deadlines to be met—just like anywhere else.

"This job is almost always interesting, though, and there's almost always something else to find out about an individual animal or group of animals. I usually work full-time (forty hours) but often stay late or come in early or on my days off to help out. The work atmosphere for the most part is pretty relaxed. Most everyone here really enjoys what they are doing and are self-motivated, so we have a pretty good team.

"What I like most is observing and learning about animals, discovering what their likes and dislikes are and what makes them thrive. I also enjoy helping to provide the public with an enjoyable and informative setting that lends to their appreciation and respect for animals. I would have to say that the hardest aspect of this job is losing an animal. We are a small zoo and we know our animals pretty well, so it's never easy. Also, we are in Texas, so the summers can be extremely hot and dry and not at all pleasant. I also do not like it when certain members of the public feel the need to torment our animals."

A WORD OF ADVICE

"Education and experience are both important. Most zoos today want at least two years of college focusing on classes in the natural sciences. If you can't get paid experience, volunteer or intern, if possible. Anywhere working with animals is helpful, but exotics have special needs, so experience with them is a plus. Be well-rounded. Zoo employees need skills such as working with and talking to the public, computer literacy, time management, and handling basic tools, not just animal experience.

"Also, join professional organizations such as the American Association of Zookeepers or the American Zoo and Aquarium Association to know what is happening in the field."

CHAPTER 4

ANIMAL BEHAVIORISTS

Many zoos either hire animal behaviorists or work with consultants to train zookeepers how to handle and interact well with the animals.

More and more zoos operate open-park facilities, as opposed to keeping animals in cement-floored cages. Animal behaviorists teach zoo owners about the needs of the different animals, for example, which animals can be kept in the same park space together and which must be separated.

The ideal animal behaviorist is someone who has experience handling animals and who is professionally trained in the areas of the scientific analysis of behavior, as well as being trained to counsel people about animals.

THE QUALIFICATIONS YOU'LL NEED

The ability to think critically is probably one of the most valuable assets an animal behaviorist should have. That also includes the ability to evaluate—to be able to tell what the results you see mean and to assess them without reference to your personal prejudice system.

Most animal behaviorists earn a doctorate degree in animal behavior programs in university psychology or zoology departments. They also must combine hands-on experience with their research interests.

FIRSTHAND ACCOUNT

Mary Lee Nitschke, Animal Behaviorist

Mary Lee Nitschke has a Ph.D. in comparative developmental psychobiology from Michigan State University and more than thirty years experience in this exciting field. In addition to the many hats she wears, Dr. Nitschke is also a consultant to the Metro Washington Park Zoo in Portland, Oregon. Dr. Nitschke explains: "The Washington Park Zoo employs a full-time animal behaviorist. I work on a consulting basis with her, doing training seminars for zookeepers on how to interact with and handle animals.

"I also give talks on wolf-dog crosses because the zoo gets questions about them all the time. The zoo has wolves, so people come with their concerns about their own pets. The Northwest is a hotbed for people owning wolves as pets. It's pretty hard on everyone, though it doesn't keep people from doing it. In a wolf-dog cross, the biggest problem I see professionally is the quality of life for that animal. If it's high percentage wolf, it's likely to be terrified of people. The second problem is unpredictability. We have no way of knowing when the wolf part is going to be operative and when the dog part is. These wolf-dog crosses have a rap very similar to pit bulls and rottweilers. It's not the same problem at all, but it looks like the same problem because they maul children frequently.

"I also do training with the zookeepers, teaching them how to manage animals in the zoo environment and how to understand and use operant behavior and clicker training. The animal is trained to click a bar that will deliver food to it as a reward. One of my colleagues was working with an ape that was diabetic and needed to have a blood sample drawn every day. Through clicker training, she taught the chimp to put its arm in a sleeve outside the cage and grasp a bar so that the blood sample could be taken quickly and efficiently without anybody being endangered. The reward was food and the animal was fine about it.

"Another one she did was to teach an elephant to present its feet for cleaning through the fence. This was an aggressive male elephant, and nobody could go in and do this. Through operant conditioning, it was taught to hold its feet up to a little panel and then they could be cleaned that way.

"I also worked with one of their birds of prey that wouldn't allow keepers in. Basically, when keepers have a problem, they call me."

BECOMING AN ANIMAL BEHAVIORIST

"For someone who wants to become an animal behaviorist, first of all, you have to have hands-on experience. And the more time you spend observing animals and learning how to interact with them, the better off you're going to be. The second thing is that you have to get educated to learn to understand, evaluate, and think like a scientist.

"Hands-on experience is very important. I don't think this is a profession that can be done totally by theory. On the other hand, the hands-on experience can't come totally from trial and error methods.

"I think the best route is to take a lot of experimental courses—psychology or in other fields. Some anthropology courses do a good job of preparing people. There are disciplines of animal behavior, both within psychology and zoology. I think that a good psychology background is important, not just for experimental psych, but if you take a major in psychology in almost any school in the country, you will have to take experimental psychology and statistics. Applied statistics is something I use on a daily basis. I'll give you an example. Every time a client comes to see me with a behavioral situation, in my mind I run that situation through a statistical analysis and can then give the probable reasons for why that behavior is occuring. My training and my knowledge of animal behavior allows me to put that situation in a framework instantly."

In addition to her zoo consulting work, Dr. Nitschke is a full-time, tenured, full professor in the psychology department at Linfield College in Portland, Oregon. There she teaches a variety of courses from Applied Animal Behavior and Human Animal Relationships, to People Pet Partnerships in Health Care.

She is also owner of Animal School, Incorporated (in Beaverton, Oregon), and through private consultations and classes, provides clients with help in solving pet behavior problems.

Here is an example of the kind of problems she sees. "Recently a fellow came in with a six-year-old bulldog mix. It looked an awful lot like a pit bull. It was a big dog, ninety pounds, and he had bitten seven people. I went through each bite. Some of these bites were almost to be expected because they resulted from inappropriate behavior on the part of the owner. In one instance the owner sent a plumber carrying a pipe into the dog's territory without announcing him. Well, he already knew the dog was territorial and didn't usually admit strangers. I don't count that bite. That was to be expected. In another instance, a teenage boy had been playing with the dog, then turned very abruptly and jumped on his bike. The dog went for him. Given this particular dog, the probability of that happening was pretty high and when you add all those bites up, the probability that the dog will bite again is also very high. Putting the dog to sleep is one of the major options I counseled the owner about, but you can't make that decision for the client. My job in that situation is to say, 'here are the likely scenarios—what will happen if you do nothing or if you do this, that, or the other?'

"What he wanted from me was to give him a training program that would guarantee that the dog wouldn't bite anyone again. But there is no such program. Most of the time you're working with the person, not the animal, and that's why you must have some grounding in counseling to do this work."

In addition, Dr. Nitschke does a lot of public speaking and is also a consultant for the invisible fencing industry. "Those are the major things," Dr. Nitschke explains, "but other things come up. I do training for the animal control people sometimes. I train them on how to handle animals, how to approach an animal when they have to go onto a property, because that's one of the most dangerous jobs in the world—going onto an animal's property and trying to pick it up."

HOW MARY LEE NITSCHKE GOT STARTED

"I grew up on the range in Texas, and my major entertainment and stimulation came from observing animals. One of my earliest memories is lying in the grass watching bobwhite quails coming to drink water in the summer. My young life was devoted to animals.

"I had spent a lot time with animals, horses especially, both showing them and training them, and when I got to college I was attracted to both engineering psychology—because I was in love with machines—and animal behavior.

"What I thought was so interesting and has fueled me throughout life in some ways, was that the theoretical stuff I was learning in college, theories of psychology and learning theory, seemed to me to be wasted if it wasn't applied. Yet my professors knew nothing about training and here we were discussing learning theory.

"And by the same token trainers knew nothing about learning theory. I couldn't imagine that both of these areas couldn't be enriched by the other, so I kept bouncing back and forth between what was going on in the training world and what was going on in learning theory in the academic world. And then when I got to grad school and discovered I could actually study this as an academic subject, too, I was just fascinated with putting that together.

"Most of my research in graduate school was aimed at the 'interspecific communication of distress.' In my dissertation I did research with bobwhite quail, jack rabbits, coyotes, blue jays, and human babies. What I was looking for was whether there was some universality of understanding of the distress call among species.

"After I graduated I taught at Michigan State University. I taught operant behavior, among other things, then I taught pet communication patterns in the veterinary school there and developmental psychobiology with a specialization in toxicology, again looking across species—what are the common elements in how toxins affect behavior in various species.

"Before I went to college I trained horses. What I later realized is that I trained every animal I came into contact with—I just didn't realize that's what I was doing.

"While I was an undergraduate, one of the things that fueled my interest in applied psychology was working in a kennel that bred and trained collies. It was really one of the golden fortunes of my life that the couple I worked for had incredible integrity and ethics about breeding. They bred for the love of the dog and could not be bought by local fashions and current fads. They knew exactly what they were breeding for—solid temperaments. I learned an incredible amount from them. I started there just cleaning dog runs, and by the time I left I was handling their line of collies professionally."

CAREER OPTIONS

Independent Trainers

Just as Dr. Nitschke does, many animal behaviorists work independently and offer training programs to pet owners. Dr. Nitschke admits that getting started can be difficult. "Your best referral sources are veterinarians. People in the United States think that veterinarians are pet gods, and so they ask them everything. If you don't have the support of the veterinarians in your local community, you're going to have a rough go of it. You have to advertise and market yourself.

Teaching

Many animal behaviorists stay in the academic world where they pass on their experience and research to university students. Just as with any professorial post, you would need your doctorate and to meet the specific requirements of the hiring department.

Animal Assisted Therapy

Another arena in which people work is animal assisted therapy. Dr. Nitschke explains: "Animal assisted therapy is where animals become part of the therapeutic process. They can be used with people who have a wide range of problems, anything from a social dog for a child who has emotional/social problems up through people who need the dog as a prosthesis, as a seeing eye, hearing ear, or seizure alert dog, for example. Animal behaviorists train animals for these roles.

Dr. Nitschke is also involved teaching others about hippotherapy and how to work with horses to help humans with neuromuscular difficulties. "I hope I'm carving out a path that will become more common as the years go by—teaching people to use animals therapeutically. One of these programs is called People Pet Partnerships in Health Care.

"Hippotherapy is horseback riding directed by a physical therapist or a kinesiologist. The movement of the horse is used as a way of stimulating neuromuscular interaction patterns with the person. My mission with this course is to teach people in the medical field some of the wonderful possibilities that are available therapeutically with animals.

"Another application is showcased by the work of Dr. Mary Birch. She works with crack babies who have no inhibitory control and scream most of the time. Those babies are very hard for the nurses to take care of. It is also very hard to impact on them in any way.

"What Dr. Birch did was use a concept called *entrainment.* You take the rhythm that's occurring in the patient, you match something to it that will correspond to that rhythm, and then you start bringing it down. She started with little, active, very flighty finches in a cage right next to the baby. The babies eventually entrained on those finches. Then, what she did was substitute the finches with birds that moved more slowly, to the point where she could finally put a chinchilla in with that baby and it would soothe the baby. It's a combination of biofeedback and animal behavior stuff and circadian rhythm stuff. There are all sorts of ways that, if you understand what is happening with the animal and its behavior, you can use it therapeutically."

Medical Research

As any animal lover knows, research using animals is a controversial subject, to say the least. However, as Dr. Nitschke points out, "anyone developing medications or procedures *for* animals is going to need the services of someone trained in evaluating behavior at some point—and should. Too often they haven't. What they've typically done is gone to veterinarians who may not have had any training in animal behavior and most often don't." An animal behaviorist working with scientists for the betterment of animals can ensure that humane practices are followed.

Training Trainers

Teaching other people how to train animals is a viable career path for animal behaviorists. Although the notion of training animals for circuses or television or film work might be abhorrent to some (there are many people who believe that animals should be left in the wild and not used for any purpose related to mankind's needs), as mentioned earlier, animals can humanely be trained to interact with humans in a therapeutic setting.

"There are a lot of folks out there who still believe that punishment is the most effective and most efficient way to train," says Dr. Nitschke. "If you get a trainer who believes that and also does not have good anger management, then the potential for abuse arises very quickly. I spend a lot of time trying to educate people about what it means to be a humane trainer. What we teach is essentially the same thing that is taught in positive parenting classes. Rewarding good behavior, ignoring the bad. That's traditional behavior modification."

INCOME FOR ANIMAL BEHAVIORISTS

Salaries would vary widely depending upon the specific work you do and the area in the country in which you live. Those working for a university would expect to be on the same pay scale as any other faculty member of the same rank and experience.

As a consultant and trainer, Mary Lee Nitschke says, "I charge everyone $90 an hour, no matter what I'm doing for them. I set that fee based on the average fee that psychologists charge in my area. And it's about to go up. I'll probably go up to $100 or a little over that. Right now, we have about twenty different classes, and the cost is about $85 to $90 for a set of six classes per student."

VACATION SCHOLARSHIPS

Vacation scholarships are available through the Association for the Study of Animal Behaviour for undergraduates to undertake supervised research projects lasting from one to eight weeks during academic vacations under the auspices of institutions of higher education.

Undergraduates may also apply for scholarships for research to be carried out in the period immediately following graduation.

Awards will not be granted for work that is part of a degree program. Projects must fall within the field of animal behavior.

The scholarship will offer an amount toward living expenses for the student and an amount toward research project expenses for the participating institution. The amounts awarded are calculated on the basis of a weekly rate, which is reviewed annually. In 1996 these rates were £75 per week towards living expenses and £25 per week towards research expenses.

To obtain an application and other pertinent information contact:

Professor Peter Hepper
Secretary of the ASAB Grants Committee
Department of Psychology
The Queen's University
Belfast BT9 7BL, Northern Ireland, UK

Project proposals should accompany the application form.

CHAPTER 5

ZOO VETERINARY STAFF

Zoo veterinarians, assisted by veterinary technicians, are responsible for all phases of animal health, including preventive medicine. All veterinarians, no matter the setting, examine, diagnose, and treat animals for any type of medical problem. Although some have a general practice treating all kinds of animals, most work with either small pets or with large animals such as horses, swine, sheep, and cattle.

Only a small number of vets are employed by zoos and aquariums.

VETERINARY SPECIALISTS

Just as medical doctors have areas of specialization, so do veterinarians. Although most go into general practice, others specialize in, for example, veterinary ophthalmology, cardiology, orthopedics, or specialized surgery.

Relief Veterinarians

Relief veterinarians function much as substitute teachers do. They work for different practices on an on-call basis, filling in for vacationing vets or during emergencies. They're usually paid for the day, with earnings varying from $150 to $300, depending on how much experience they have and the area of the country in which they practice.

Research and Food Safety Inspection

Veterinarians contribute to human as well as animal health. Some vets engage in research to prevent and treat diseases in humans. They also help prevent the outbreak of rabies or other diseases that can be transmitted to humans and may quarantine animals or perform autopsies when necessary.

Veterinarians who are meat inspectors examine slaughtering and processing plants, check live animals and carcasses for disease, and enforce government food purity and sanitation regulations.

SETTINGS FOR VETERINARIANS

Most vets work in animal clinics or hospitals, but some also work for zoos, the government, public health, universities, and racetracks. Relief veterinarians have a variety of offices for which they work, and vets also can choose to travel further afield, wherever their services are needed.

TRAINING FOR VETERINARIANS

All vets must be licensed, and to become licensed, vets must have a Doctor of Veterinary Medicine degree (D.V.M. or V.M.D.) from an accredited college of veterinary medicine and pass a state board exam.

For research and/or teaching positions, a master's or Ph.D. is usually required. For a specialty certification, a veterinarian must complete a three-year residency program and pass an examination.

The D.V.M. degree requires a minimum of six years of college, two of preveterinary study (physical and biological sciences) and four of vet school. But because admission to a school of veterinary medicine is very competitive, most successful applicants have completed four years of undergraduate work before they apply.

EARNINGS FOR VETERINARIANS

According to the most recent figures collected by the American Veterinary Medical Association, the average starting salary of 1991 veterinary medical college graduates was $27,858. The average income of veterinarians in private practice was $63,069. Those averages have probably risen somewhat since then.

The average annual salary for veterinarians in the federal government in nonsupervisory, supervisory, and managerial positions was $50,482 in 1993.

Zoo veterinarians usually make much less money than those vets established in private practice. Whereas a private practitioner can earn anywhere from $100,000 on up, a zoo vet's salary could range from $30,000 to $40,000 a year.

VETERINARIAN ASSISTANTS AND TECHNICIANS

Just as medical doctors rely heavily on nurses and other medical personnel, so do veterinarians depend on assistants and technicians. These workers are a valuable asset to any practice.

Some assistants and technicians are successful landing a job without formal training and are taught the skills they need on the job. However, many vets these days, or the zoos they work for, require their technicians to have gone through a formal training program. (The address for information on education for vet techs is listed in Appendix A.)

In addition, a vet tech can expect his or her salary to increase with an official diploma or certificate.

Veterinary hospitals and zoos employ three types of caretakers: veterinary technician, veterinary assistant, and animal attendant. Veterinary technicians, also known as animal health technicians, are the most skilled. They keep records, take specimens, perform laboratory tests, prepare animals and instruments for surgery, take and develop radiographs, dress wounds, and assist veterinarians with examinations and surgery. However, they do not diagnose ailments, prescribe medication, or perform surgery.

Veterinary assistants feed and bathe animals, administer medication as prescribed by a veterinarian, and help veterinarians and the veterinary technicians treat animals. For example, the assistant may hold the animal while the technician gives it an injection.

Animal attendants clean cages, exercise animals, and monitor the animals for symptoms of illnesses. This is the most basic job and is frequently performed by part-time workers.

Licensing for Vet Techs

Forty-two states require veterinary technicians to be licensed; this is the only animal caretaker position requiring licensure. Licensure requirements in most states include graduation from an accredited animal technology program. There are approximately sixty-three associate programs and five bachelor's degree programs accredited by the American Veterinary Medicine Association.

Courses include animal pharmacology, veterinary physiology and anatomy, animal care and management, radiography, anesthetic nursing and monitoring, parasitology, animal husbandry, chemistry, biology, applied mathematics, communications, and the humanities.

In states without education requirements for veterinary technicians, veterinarians may employ applicants with a strong science background and train them on the job; however, most veterinarians prefer graduates of formal academic programs.

There are no formal education requirements for animal attendants and veterinary assistants in veterinary facilities. They are trained on the job.

ZOO MEDICINE

In a zoo setting, a vet's and a vet tech's job differs greatly from the responsibilities found in a small animal practice. Vets and their assistants might see some animals inside the confines of the hospital, but most contact is done on the grounds of the zoo, for spot checks, treatment of minor conditions, parasite control, and general maintenance. Only when necessary would a large animal be transported to the hospital grounds.

THE ZOO NURSERY

In addition to providing both preventative and emergency medical care to zoo animals, many vets and vet techs are involved with the zoo nursery.

With new special diets and more scientific care, many more baby animals are being born and raised in zoos than in the past. If a mother is unable to care for her newborn, or if the baby is not doing well, staff members may decide to move the baby and hand raise it in the nursery.

In many zoos, the nursery is a glass-walled room that allows visitors to observe the animal infants. After repeated visits, observers can note changes in the animals' growth and development. The nursery staff often posts records where visitors can see them. These charts document weight gain and the animal's medical history.

FIRSTHAND ACCOUNTS

Dr. Christine Miller, Veterinarian

Dr. Christine Miller is the staff veterinarian at Metrozoo in Miami. She is responsible for a collection of about 400 to 500 animals. She is the only vet on staff and works with the assistance of one vet tech (see the following interview with Jacky Shaw) and one hospital assistant.

DR. CHRISTINE MILLER'S BACKGROUND

"I am an animal person and I have always been interested in animals. Zoos always appealed to me. They have a variety of animals, and I find the natural history and the behavior of animals fascinating. As opposed to domestic animals, wild animals are a little more pure, a little more challenging, a little more varied. If I hadn't gotten into vet school, I probably still would have pursued some other avenue of zoo work or work with wildlife. I wanted to be a vet all my life. I am interested in science and getting a medical background seemed like a reasonable thing to do. I like figuring out puzzles and solving things, and, of course, being of some help to the animals, too.

"I attended Cornell University, in Ithaca, New York, as an undergraduate, then went on to vet school at Cornell as well, graduating there in 1985.

"After I graduated, I did two more years in pathology training. One of those years I did at Cornell, the other in Melbourne, Australia. I chose pathology specifically because I wanted the background, not because I was interested in pursuing a career in pathology. There is only a limited amount of knowledge about the species we keep. The field is growing every day, of course, but to work with individuals animals, I felt it was important to know everything about them, including why they died and how they were made. I found that a pathology background would be useful, not only because I can examine the animals I treat and learn more about them when they die so that information isn't wasted, but because that kind of background lets you know more about what is normal in anatomy and surgery.

"When I got back from Australia I taught at Cornell for a year. From there I needed to get back into clinical medicine, so I did an internship at Colorado State University with a combination exotic animal and small animal medicine and surgery. In addition to the usual pets, I worked with exotic pets such as turtles, guinea pigs, ferrets, rabbits. I also worked in wildlife rehabilitation, mostly with birds of prey.

"After I finished my internship I was hired at Indianapolis Zoo as an associate veterinarian to help a friend of mine. Before I actually got started, she quit, so I ended up being the only vet there. But it was considered a temporary position for the year I worked there, and when I learned about the position opening here in Miami through a friend who used to work here, I applied. The job was also advertised through the American Association of Zoo Veterinarians, and you have to be active in that if you want to know what's going on. They have a newsletter and conferences and everyone talks to everyone else. We pick up the phone and call a colleague and say, 'Look, I've got a bear that's doing this weird thing. Have you ever seen it before?' And while you are talking to someone about those kinds of things, you also learn what the scoop is, where the jobs are opening up. I went through the usual process, sending in a resume, and then I flew here for an interview. It's just like applying for a job in any field. You need your letters of recommendation, and because this is a county job, you take your drug testing and your blood tests and go through all the paperwork. The whole process was speeded up, though. It took only about a month because they really needed to get someone on board here quickly. The vet had already left before they advertised the position officially."

A TYPICAL DAY

"I come to work at 7:30 A.M. and open up the hospital and make sure all the animals in quarantine are doing well. Unfortunately, because we are understaffed, two days a week I start cleaning and feeding all the animals. If not, I start working on the plans for the day. If I'm doing an immobilization procedure for an animal that will be transported or if I need to change bandages or whatever, I do that first. At 9:00 I greet the keepers in the hay barn and find out if anything happened overnight. We work through all the animals that need to be seen, I do the paperwork, grab some lunch, return phone calls.

"I run into every situation imaginable with the animals. I deal with trauma caused by a cage mate or trauma from something the animals did to themselves because they got spooked and ran into a wall. Or maybe a visitor threw something at them. We run into all sorts of diseases. Babies get everything from pneumonia to malformations. The old animals get diseases like cancer or heart, liver, or kidney failure, and in between they get infections or abscesses. You name it, if it goes wrong, I treat it. There is nothing different between animals and people except for some of the politics of the situation. Animals aren't going to talk back to me or sue me for malpractice. But they can try to refuse treatment, obviously.

"I work with everything from little lizards that weigh just a few grams to elephants and rhinos and tigers and bears. The keepers who take care of the animals assist me when I am out in the field. The majority of my work is done in the zoo, not in the hospital. For example, if we have a lion with a toothache, we wouldn't bring him into the hospital. We have special facilities meant to handle those animals. We have a hallway that the animals traverse as they leave their cages and go out to the exhibit for the day. In that hallway we have an area that we can close doors on that shuts it down into a small room. The back wall of that hallway is built so that it can be pulled tight against the front wall. We call that a squeeze cage. The animal is brought into this area and positioned so he can't really move around a lot. Then I can give him a shot or take a blood sample through the bars of that hallway. If I have to do something in their mouth or if I have to take an x-ray, then I would tranquilize them. But for a blood sample or vaccination it isn't necessary. It's over in a few minutes and they're out the door."

THE UPSIDES AND DOWNSIDES

"What I enjoy most in my work is the challenge of diagnosing cases or figuring out how to treat an animal when the animal doesn't want to be treated. Also, the same holds true for a unique animal that requires my improvisational skills in order to come up with a method of dealing with it. I like almost all the animals and I like the variety, but my favorite is working with the babies. Everybody likes working with babies. It can be such a heartbreak, though. You get so attached to them. If they are sick and you are trying to pull them through, you feed all your emotions into them, but they can die anyway. But at the same time, if things go right and you're able to save them, it can be the most rewarding experience. You just feel wonderful.

"Other downsides are the politics, the budgeting, the paperwork drudgery, the long hours. A lot of the times you don't mind the long hours, but there are times when you've just gotten home and you want to relax or go see a movie, and then you get called and you have to come back in.

"There are injuries to contend with, too, in this business. I think that any vet who works with animals is going to face a major injury in his or her life. If you work with animals everyday, sooner or later you're going to get hurt. If you work with zoo animals, your chances of being seriously injured are much higher. Or if you work with horses. You might work with 70,000 horses over the years and they are all wonderful. But there's always that one that can get away from you and nail you with a foot. We all take precautions and we're all careful in our jobs, but you run the risk when you work with animals that are capable of killing people.

I've had a partial amputation of my thumb from a chimpanzee. It wasn't a life-threatening injury, but it was significant just the same. People are really wrong when they think of chimps as being friendly animals. Chimps can be incredibly aggressive. They are very close to people behaviorally in many ways. They can be jealous, aggressive, nasty, cranky. And we don't put them in a situation where they are going to like veterinarians. When I show up, there's usually some pain or discomfort involved for them. They associate me with a shot, not as someone who really cares. They want to bite me and spit at me and throw feces at me. No matter what my intentions are, they don't want me around."

SALARIES FOR ZOO VETS

"Private practitioners have the capacity to earn much more money than zoo vets. But as Metrozoo goes, I am paid much better than many other zoo veterinarians are. Many zoo veterinarians are paid relatively meager wages. I don't mean they are starving, but the salaries are not glamorous. Probably the average zoo veterinarian is making between $30,000 and $38,000 a year. When I started in Indianapolis, I was only making $19,000 a year. Now a new zoo vet might start in the mid to high twenties. Someone with ten years or so of experience can expect only in the high thirties. You don't go into the zoo business to make money. You really have to like what you're doing. If you want to make money as a vet, you have to go into private practice. And in some cases, you have to go into a high risk practice, working with horses or in neighborhoods where there is money to be spent. By high risk, I mean there's a higher risk of being sued."

A WORD OF ADVICE

"You really have to want to be a vet even before you choose zoos as the setting in which you'll work. Again, you have to realize you're not going to get rich and that you'll put in long hours.

Plus, the field is very competitive, so you have to be persistent. There aren't a lot of jobs available out there.

"At the same time, if you go for it, it is everything it's cracked up to be. It's a challenging and rewarding career. It is definitely a career, not a job, and it can be physically and mentally very stressful. But it's what I always wanted to do, and I am glad that I have."

Jacky Shaw, Veterinary Technician

Jacky Shaw is a vet tech at Metrozoo in Miami working alongside Dr. Christine Miller, profiled above. She has been at Metrozoo since 1983.

JACKY SHAW'S BACKGROUND

"I always have liked animals. I studied animal husbandry and dairy science at the Lancashire County Institute of Agriculture in England (I am from England), dealing mostly with cows, sheep, and goats. I earned a national diploma in dairying. Comparing it to U.S. training, it is beyond an associate's degree but not quite a bachelor's. The program offers more than the U.S. vet tech programs here.

"After I finished, I went to Jamaica and taught animal husbandry there for three years. We lived on a farm, and we've always had animals. I then went to Canada and worked on a beef farm for three years. When I came here to Miami I worked at first with a local dog and cat veterinarian for three years. I saw the job at the zoo advertised, and so I applied and was chosen. There were about fifty other applicants, so I was very lucky."

JACKY SHAW'S DUTIES AT METROZOO

"I assist the vet in anything we do. That means I help with anesthesia, surgery, and I do parasite control. We check every animal in the zoo for parasites about once a month. I also dispense medication and I do blood work. I sterilize all the instruments, too. Then there is the documentation. I input everything into the computer. And there is a lot of laundry to do, clothes and sheets and blankets and towels. We use sheets in the hospital; right now we are hand raising a baby bear and he always needs clean sheets, he makes such a mess. Laundry is a large percentage of my day it seems.

"I work with anything and everything. I come in in the morning and never know what's going to happen. We do have a planned schedule but that can change. Dr. Miller might be working on something when I arrive, so I just dive in to help her. Maybe an animal has broken its leg or there's an unexpected C-section.

"We don't have an actual zoo nursery, but sometimes we do have a baby that comes into the hospital to be hand raised. Sometimes I'll be assigned, or sometimes Dr. Miller, or it could be one of the zookeepers who takes charge. The best situation is to keep the baby with its mother in the zoo, but sometimes the mother dies or maybe she has rejected the baby or the baby is not healthy. Then we have to step in. We bring them into the hospital to get them started on the bottle, and eventually they might go home with different staff members to spend the night. With some animals we can take them back to the herd and the keeper will come to the fence with the bottle and the baby will run up and get fed, then go back and join the others. This we do a lot with gazelles.

"We only take the small ones home, under twenty pounds. One Christmas we had a new zebu cow, a miniature Indian cow with a hump. That I got to take home with me. I have also taken a baby camel home. The little bear goes home with one of three zookeepers. He needs his middle of the night feedings so can't be left alone.

"Some days you work straight through until midnight; other days it can be low key and very quiet. But you always have to be ready for emergencies.

"First thing in the morning we check on the animals that are in the hospital. They could be sick or in quarantine. We feed and medicate them.

"About 9:30 or 10:00 we start our checks out in the field. If an animal is going to be traded to another zoo, we chemically immobilize it, check its blood, give it TB tests, then move it to our shipping pen for a couple of weeks until it's ready to go.

"I work alongside Dr. Miller in the field. In the zoo hospital we have a zookeeper/hospital manager, myself, and Dr. Miller. It's just the three of us for the entire zoo.

"We do a lot of dental work, too, root canals on tigers, for example. They are kept in cages at night and they occasionally break a tooth chewing on the bars.

"We have had a few animals with cancer. One was a tiger with a cancerous growth around her eye, and we had to take her to get radiation therapy. She is in remission now, so we are pleased about that. We have to tranquilize them, of course. We take them to people hospitals, but quietly.

"We took a baby rhino to a human hospital once a few years ago. But people assumed that we have a large CAT scan on our property. We get calls every so often from hospitals that need a CAT scan for a large person. There are people who are 500 or 600 pounds and they need the large equipment, but we don't have it. The baby rhino we were dealing with was only 90 pounds at the time.

"We also work with all the primates. We bring the gorillas in one at a time every year for an annual checkup. Every day we schedule teeth cleaning on gorillas, chimps, lions, and tigers. They can get gingivitis just like people do. The elephant zookeepers can handle the preventative care themselves. The footwork, for example. The elephants are trainable, so they will lift up their foot for the keepers.

"We probably deal with 300 to 400 animals a year. I enjoyed working with the dogs and cats, but these exotic animals are special and I enjoy the variety. I used to get very attached to the animals, but we've had a few instances where we had to euthanize an animal because it got too sick or it broke a leg and it wasn't fixable. So you have to learn to toughen yourself up. In August we had a gorilla with a heart problem. We had immobilized him to check him out, but he never woke up. It's very sad. This animal had been at the zoo for twenty years, and you get to know each other.

"But the useful thing is that when we do lose an animal, Dr. Miller performs a necropsy, and that helps you to get over the sadness. It is fascinating to see how the heart was deteriorating and the valves not working. You try to turn a negative into a positive. Also, we can contribute research for other animals with heart problems.

"A minor downside is that every time I have a wedding or social event to attend, there's an emergency and I am called in. But I bring my husband along and he thinks it's fascinating. We can go out anytime, but how often do you get to see a C-section?

"I work officially 9:00 to 5:00 Monday through Friday, but you have to be prepared to give more than that. In the summer, for example, we come in early to get work done because it's so hot during the day."

JACKY SHAW'S SALARY

"Fourteen years ago I started out at $18,000. Now I earn $30,000. It's a very good salary, and we get a lot of good benefits from the county, like medical coverage, etc."

A WORD OF ADVICE

"There are only about sixty to ninety of us vet techs in the whole country, so the chances of getting into a job like this are pretty remote. It's a good idea to volunteer; then when an opening comes up, you'll be there.

"Another tactic is to go the medical tech route. Quite a few of the larger zoos have medical technicians, technologists who were trained to work with people. But they can easily cross over to work with animals, so this could be one way to get in. The pay isn't as good, but they get the satisfaction of working with the animals.

"There are good vet tech colleges, so I'd advise you get formal training. Also, make sure you have a background working with a variety of animals. You need to have good animal sense.

"It is a fascinating job, and most in the field have no intention of leaving, so the job chances are pretty slim."

CHAPTER 6

WILDLIFE REHABILITATION

Wildlife rehabilitation is the act of taking care of injured, ill, and orphaned wild animals with the goal of releasing them into their natural habitat. An individually tailored program for each animal involves examination, diagnosis, and treatment through veterinary and hospital care, feeding, medication, physical therapy, exercise, and prerelease preparation. Releases are planned to take place during appropriate weather and seasons and are aimed for the right habitats and locations.

Those animals that are beyond help when found are humanely euthanized. Animals that cannot be released can occasionally provide valuable research information or are suitable as educational aids.

There are critics of wildlife rehabilitation. They say that nature should be allowed to take its course, with injured or ill wild animals roaming free to meet their natural fate. However, extensive research shows that most of the injured, ill, and orphaned wild animals handled by rehabilitators are distressed not because of "natural" illnesses or occurrences, but because of human interventions, some of which are accidental, some intentional, many preventable. Animals can be injured by automobiles and trains, lawn mowers, high line wires, guns and other weapons, inhumane traps, unsupervised children, lumbering activities, plate glass windows, poisons, oil spills, domestic pets, and a variety of other causes. Dedicated rehabilitation experts ease the suffering of these animals either by caring for them until they can be released or by humanely euthanizing them.

Trained rehabilitators with legal permits are an important link in the network of people and organizations helping wildlife. Not only do they care for animals and return them to the wild, they also help reduce the negative human impact on wildlife and the environment. Some rehabilitators are involved in research, captive breeding, and release-to-the-wild projects. Others are also involved in public education, exposing both children and adults to biological facts, ecological concepts, and a responsible attitude toward all living things.

HOW TO BECOME A WILDLIFE REHABILITATOR

Permits from both state and federal wildlife agencies must be obtained in order to possess or handle wildlife. This includes all birds with the exception of pigeons, European starlings, and house sparrows. In addition to the birds, permits also are required to possess the feathers and the nest.

The agencies issuing the permits require all rehabilitators to keep detailed records on all the animals they care for. These records are submitted annually to state and federal agencies. Wildlife rehabilitation facilities are also subject to sporadic site inspections.

State permit requirements vary from state to state. Some states require only an application (which includes a description of your previous experience in wildlife rehabilitation) and a licensing fee. Other states insist upon extensive training and require that applicants become certified prior to obtaining permits. Federal permits are issued by region.

To get application forms, you must contact the appropriate office in your region. It may take up to six months to obtain the necessary permits. For a list of regional offices, see Appendix C.

To become involved with an existing wildlife rehabilitation center, contact those of interest to you and volunteer your time. Larger centers with adequate budgets can occasionally take on paid employees. As a volunteer you would be in a position to know when an opportunity opens up.

WILDLIFE REHABILITATION INFORMATION

The Internet is a valuable source of information on this topic. Use any search engine and type in the words "wildlife rehabilitation." You will find information on the professional associations supporting the field (also see Appendix A for addresses and other important professional association information) as well as the following:

a directory of wildlife rehabilitation centers
profiles of centers and individual rehabbers
tips for professional rehabbers
laws regarding wildlife
health hazards
conferences and workshops
supply centers
question and answer forums
permit information

Many books and pamphlets have also been published on the subject. See Appendix B for more information.

CLOSE-UP: LA GUARDAR INC. WILDLIFE REHABILITATION AND EDUCATION CENTER

Permitted by the U.S. Fish and Wildlife Service and the Florida Game and Fresh Water Fish Commission, La Guardar Inc. seeks a positive and cooperative relationship with all efforts to conserve our natural environment and resources.

Wildlife entering the center are examined and treated by the volunteer staff in cooperation with local veterinarians. They enter the rehabilitation program after being monitored and considered ready. Injured and orphaned wildlife are cared for until they can be released back in the wild in the vicinity where they were found, or to a suitable habitat where they naturally occur.

Wildlife that recover but are permanently impaired are housed and are used for public educational programs. Or, they are given to acceptable zoological parks. Those that do not survive are donated to public educational or scientific institutions.

La Guardar Inc., in Webster, Florida, is publicly funded by memberships, donations, grants, bequests, and fund-raisers. It receives no governmental support and has no paid employees or officers.

FIRSTHAND ACCOUNT

Shelby Rodney Carter, Assistant Curator, Vice President, and Co-Founder of La Guardar Inc.

Shelby Carter (Rod) is the founder of La Guardar Inc. This is the account of how he got started:

"In the late spring of 1986, a gentleman entered our real estate and construction office. He inquired of my wife if she knew of anyone who could help an injured barred owl. On his way to work he had hit the owl with his car. The owl was in shock and had an injured wing.

"The upset gentleman was late for work, but he waited while my wife called the Florida Game and Fresh Water Fish Commission. A representative informed my wife of a wildlife rehabilitation center located in St. Petersburg, Florida. She also informed her that the possession of even the feather of a bird of prey carried a stiff penalty, unless there was a federal and state permit involved.

"My wife and I owned a small cattle ranch at the time and were experienced in caring for animals. She knew that the owl would not survive the two-hour journey to the wildlife center. She informed the Florida Game and Fresh Water Fish representative that she intended to care for the owl and asked her to send the necessary permit application. The representative agreed and gave my wife the address to apply for a federal permit.

"Relieved of his burden of the injured owl, the gentleman left a donation, along with the owl, and departed.

"Thus began the adventure of caring for injured and orphaned wildlife. My plans on retiring the following year to sail around the world ended.

"Word got around that my wife cared for wildlife, and a year later we were knee-deep in injured and orphaned wildlife. Lack of space and funding were becoming a problem.

"On five acres near our ranch, I had begun construction in early 1985 on what was to be our retirement home. It was a 1,200-square-foot building, with a kitchen, bedroom, bath, storage, and double carport. Our plan was to duplicate the building on an acre we owned in the mountains of western North Carolina. We planned to spend the seasons, when we were not sailing, at the two small homes.

"I enclosed the double carport and the building became a wildlife rehabilitation center. We sold the ranch and moved into the building along with the animals. A year later, I had completed a 1,500-square-foot home tied to the wildlife center by a foyer. During that year, I built numerous habitats to house recuperating wildlife.

"Beginning in early 1987, I set up La Guardar Inc., a nonprofit, tax-exempt, Florida corporation. The corporation is structured to provide immediate and continuing care to injured and orphaned Florida native wildlife. It is governed by a board, elected by the active membership. Officers are appointed by the board.

La Guardar is Spanish for "the keep," which is the center of a castle where things of value are gathered in times of peril. We believe that all wildlife is vital to the ecosystem, which is the very heart of all life."

THE UPSIDES AND DOWNSIDES

"A career in wildlife rehabilitation, while it may not be very rewarding monetarily, is in so many other ways," Rod explains. "The primary reward is the joy of seeing an animal released back into the wild after recovering from injuries. You also get to meet a special class of people who volunteer their time to care for wildlife. Knowing that you are giving something of value back is very rewarding. Wildlife, while they can not speak to thank us, honor us with their spirit, antics, tenacity, and beauty.

"The downside is, without a doubt, euthanasia. But taking the life from an injured animal, while difficult, is sometimes the kindest thing we can do.

"Other downsides—we never get to travel. Wildlife require constant attention. The hours are sometimes hard to manage. Rescuing an animal late on a cold rainy night has its drawbacks."

THE DAY'S WORK

"As assistant curator, I am involved in rescue and release, accounting, fund-raising, grant writing, habitat construction, and maintenance. I also edit a quarterly newsletter. The hours are long, normally twelve to fourteen hours a day. But the work is not stressful and it is never boring. Spring is our busy time of the year because of the many orphaned wildlife.

"We house a variety of permanent impaired wildlife, including eagles, hawks, kestrels, owls, songbirds, bobcats, opossum, raccoons, skunks, and reptiles. They require feeding morning and evening. During the day, habitats have to be repaired and cleaned and water provided. Not always a pleasant chore.

"I have learned that animals are not just species, but individuals. They have personalities much like Homo sapiens. For instance, Big Bob, a bobcat that we rescued, was used to train dogs to hunt. He had been wired through his hind legs so he could not escape. However, he managed to escape his tormentors and was found on the front porch of a home.

"Big Bob was found with numerous bites on his hind quarter, his legs were torn, and his hearing was impaired by mites that had eaten most of his ears. Because of his diet during captivity, he had developed fatty liver disease.

"It was nearly a year before Big Bob recovered from his injuries. He remains on a low fat diet. I have observed him converse with several of our domestic cats through the wire of his habitat. He remains proud and wild. He accepts his fate with dignity and provides me with many hours of pleasure watching him—when he is not aware.

"We also have two young American eagles that were blown from their nest during the storm of the century. Their wings were damaged beyond repair. They are being trained to the glove for educational programs.

"The eagles, Stormy and Windy, are a joy to watch. They are like children growing up. They play with pinecones, limbs, and their food. In their pond, they bathe and argue with each other. Brother and sister, but she dominates. After four years their white feathers are just coming in. They are proud birds.

"I honestly would pay someone to let me work with wildlife."

A WORD OF ADVICE

"If you are interested in wildlife rehabilitation, you should volunteer at an established center. After you gain some experience, you may be able to find paid employment with some of the larger centers. Contact your local game commission or wildlife rehabilitators association. Also, check out wildlife rehabilitation on the Internet.

WILDLIFE PROTECTION LAWS

The U.S. government has enacted numerous laws to protect our natural resources. Listed below are the laws regarding wildlife.

The Migratory Bird Treaty Act
The Endangered Species Act
The Eagle Protection Act
The Wild Bird Conservation Act
The Migratory Bird Treaty Act

As an example of what these laws entail, the Endangered Species Act is described below.

The Endangered Species Act (ESA), which was passed in 1973 and reauthorized in 1988, regulates a range of activities affecting plants and animals designated as endangered or threatened. An "endangered species" is defined as an animal or plant listed by regulation as being in danger of extinction.

A "threatened species" is any animal or plant that is likely to become endangered within the foreseeable future.

The act prohibits the following activities involving endangered species:

- importing into or exporting from the United States
- taking (which includes harassing, harming, pursuing, hunting, shooting, wounding, trapping, killing, capturing, or collecting) within the United States and its territorial seas
- possessing, selling, delivering, carrying, transporting, or shipping any such species unlawfully taken within the United States or on the high seas
- delivering, receiving, carrying, transporting, or shipping in interstate or foreign commerce in the course of a commercial activity
- selling or offering for sale in interstate or foreign commerce

Prohibitions apply to endangered species, their parts, and products. Most of these restrictions also apply to species listed as threatened unless the species qualifies for an exception. The act also requires that wildlife be imported or exported through designated ports and that special declarations be filed. If the value of wildlife imported and/or exported is $25,000 per year or more, importers and exporters must be licensed.

EXCEPTIONS

Permits may be granted for scientific or propagation purposes or for economic hardship situations involving endangered or threatened species.

PENALTIES

Violators of the Endangered Species Act are subject to fines of up to $100,000 and one year imprisonment. Organizations found in violation may be fined up to $200,000. Fish, wildlife, plants, and vehicles and equipment used in violations may be subject to forfeiture.

REWARDS

Individuals providing information leading to a civil penalty or criminal conviction may be eligible for cash rewards.

CHAPTER 7

AQUARIUM CAREERS

Although the term *aquarium* can refer to a receptacle, such as a goldfish bowl or small home tank in which fish and other aquatic organisms are kept by hobbyists, it is also used to refer to a building in which many different forms of aquatic life either are put on display for the public or are used in research. Many public aquariums are found in indoor facilities, but there are some open-air aquariums in places where the climate permits.

There are two basic types of aquariums. The differences stem from the type of water used and the kinds of fish and other creatures kept in them. Marine, or seawater, aquariums hold creatures found in the ocean, and freshwater aquariums hold creatures from rivers and lakes.

HISTORY OF AQUARIUMS

Aquariums date back thousands of years. The Sumerians of Mesopotamia were the first known to keep fish in artificial ponds at least 4,500 years ago. Other early cultures involved with aquariums include the Egyptians, Assyrians, Chinese, Japanese, and Romans.

These first aquariums provided both entertainment and a place to breed fish for market. The Chinese were the earliest to begin breeding ornamental fish for keeping in small containers. The goldfish, a type of carp, was one result of their efforts.

In the 1800s, once the relationship between oxygen, animals, and plants became known, aquarium keeping became a well-established science. London's Regent's Park can boast of the first public aquarium, which opened in 1853. Later aquariums began appearing in Berlin, Naples, and Paris. There were forty-five public or commercial aquariums throughout the world by the early 1900s. The worldwide depression slowed subsequent growth, and few new, large aquariums were built until after World War II.

AQUARIUM DESIGN AND MAINTENANCE

Huge exhibition tanks in public aquariums are often set into the walls. Thousands of fish of many species share settings of rock, sand, or coral that imitate their natural habitats. Aquarium staff design and place signs or charts that indicate the popular and scientific names of the specimens and where they originate.

Glass is considered the safest construction material for aquariums. Other materials, such as certain plastics and adhesives, can be poisonous to water-breathing animals. With marine animals, it is even more important to take care with construction materials because saltwater can dissolve metals and produce substances that are toxic.

Large public aquariums are particularly difficult to maintain because the requirements of many different aquatic animals must be taken into account. These aquariums usually require a number of accessories and sophisticated support systems, including such items as filters, air pumps, lights, and heaters.

JOBS TITLES WITHIN AQUARIUMS

The collections in large public aquariums require a variety of specialists to maintain them: engineers, accountants, animal trainers, curators, aquarists, and biologists. What follows is a sampling of typical animal-related jobs found in aquariums.

Aquarists

Aquarists are the frontline people who take care of the exhibits. One of the primary skills an aquarist must bring to the job is nationally recognized certification as a scuba diver. In addition to maintaining and cleaning the exhibits, aquarists are the primary people responsible for stocking them. Depending on the size of the exhibit, an aquarist will do a lot of diving both inside the exhibit tanks as well as out of the building, collecting in local waters.

There are several aquarist rankings, and the job titles will vary depending upon the particular institution. In general they are: aquarist-in-training, trained aquarist, senior aquarist, and supervisor. At the New England Aquarium, profiled later in this chapter, aquarists are also divided into two main categories: diving aquarists and gallery aquarists. Diving aquarists dive into the large tank exhibit to maintain the health of the fish and to take care of the exhibit in general.

Gallery aquarists are in charge of smaller exhibits, but many more of them. Gallery aquarists also spend time in the water, but they aren't in a wet suit every day. Every one gets wet; some get wet more often than others.

All aquarists go on collecting trips and use their diving skills in that capacity, too.

Aquarists also need fishing and boat-handling skills.

At some institutions, as aquarists become more experienced, they are given opportunities to develop their own special niches, getting involved in research or conservation projects as well as participating in collecting trips.

Curator

An aquarium's general curator takes care of all husbandry matters. Under this top position's jurisdiction would fall curators responsible for different areas of an aquarium's operation. For example, an aquarium could have curators of fish, marine mammals, exhibit design, research, and conservation. These curator positions often involve more administrative than hands-on duties.

Trainer

At some institutions, trainers would follow rankings similar to aquarists: assistant trainer (or trainer-in-training), trainer, senior trainer, and supervisor. Trainers are responsible for the care of their animals and the exhibits as well as teaching medical behaviors, presentation behaviors, and research behaviors. For more information see the firsthand account of a trainer later in this chapter.

Veterinarian

Every institution runs a veterinarian services department; the number of staff involved depends on the size of the facility and its budget. Turn to Chapter 5 for more information on veterinary careers in zoos and aquariums.

Other departments within aquariums are similar to those found in zoos and museums. They are: conservation, design, research, education, marketing, and public relations.

SALARIES FOR AQUARISTS

Salaries vary depending upon the institution's funding and the size of its budget. An entry-level aquarist would start from the high teens to the low twenties. Senior aquarists would move up the ladder in the neighborhood of $27,000 to $30,000 a year. A supervisor could earn in the mid thirties to low forties.

SALARIES FOR TRAINERS

Entry-level salaries begin in the twenties and go up from there. A trainer can advance quickly and at the assistant curator level earn between $30,000 and $45,000, depending upon experience.

SALARIES FOR CURATORS

Salaries for curators range from the mid forties to the mid sixties, depending upon the numbers of years of accrued experience.

BECOMING A CERTIFIED DIVER

There are four or five nationally and internationally recognized certifying agencies. Future aquarists are responsible for obtaining this training and should do so in most instances before applying for an aquarist's position. Many university physical education departments offer diver training. It can also be pursued privately through the YMCA or local dive shops. There full services are offered, including equipment use as well as training. A glance through the phone book will point you in the right direction.

Additional job titles and their descriptions are presented in the following section.

CLOSE-UP: NEW ENGLAND AQUARIUM, BOSTON

Built in 1969, Boston's New England Aquarium is one of the premiere showcases for the display of marine life and habitats. Its mission is to "present, promote, and protect the world of water." These goals are carried out through exhibits and through education, conservation, and research programs.

Exhibits showcase the diversity, importance, and beauty of aquatic life and habitats and highlight aquatic conservation issues of importance. The centerpiece for the aquarium is the 187,000-gallon Giant Ocean Tank Caribbean Coral Reef Exhibit, which rises through four stories of the facility. Visitors are afforded a multi-angle view of sea turtles, sharks, moray eels, and the other tropical fish that live inside. The Ocean Tray, which holds 131,000 gallons of water and surrounds the Great Ocean Tank on the ground floor, is home to a colony of black-footed and rockhopper penguins.

In a floating pavilion adjacent to the aquarium, sea lion presentations of natural and learned behaviors are featured every day. Harbor seals reside in the outdoor pool on the aquarium's plaza. Some of these seals were found as orphaned pups along the New England coast and have been cared for by skilled aquarium biologists as part of their rescue and rehabilitation program. Through this program, aquarium staff work with distressed or injured marine animals in the wild such as whales, dolphins, sea turtles, and seals. Their goals are to rescue, rehabilitate, and, whenever possible, release the animals back into the wild.

Other research programs include working to preserve the endangered red-bellied turtle species and to help increase the declining population of black-footed penguins.

The New England Aquarium also offers a whale-watch program and a "Science at Sea" harbor tour boat.

To maintain such a range of exhibits and programs, the New England Aquarium relies on the skills and experience of a variety of professionals.

Career Opportunities at the New England Aquarium

The New England Aquarium is currently carrying out major expansion plans, increasing the size of its facility and also the scope of its mission—to focus on communicating the importance of conservation through educational and research efforts.

These expansion plans are creating a significant increase in career opportunities for qualified people with a wide range of skills, education, and experience.

Some of the departments anticipated to have openings include, but are not limited to, finance, development, animal husbandry, education, conservation, design, maintenance, research, public relations, food services, visitor services, and retail sales. Those interested in working for the New England Aquarium should send a resume and cover letter indicating a specific interest or position applied for to:

Associate Director, Human Resources
New England Aquarium
Central Wharf
Boston, MA 02110-3399

The New England Aquarium requests that job applicants do not telephone. Job openings are regularly listed in the newspaper and through the professional associations.

Sample Jobs at the New England Aquarium

These job positions are presented here to give you an idea of the type of work available at the New England Aquarium and the qualifications you would need to be considered. It is by no means an inclusive list. Additional aquarium job titles and duties are described earlier in this chapter.

ASSISTANT TRAINER

Department: Marine Mammals

Reports to: Assistant Curator of Marine Mammals

Hours: 40 hours, weekdays, weekends, holidays

Qualifications: Minimum high school graduate; B.A./B.S. in psychology or animal behavior preferred. A minimum of six months' experience handling/caring for marine mammals. Scuba certification required.

Responsibilities: Responsible for the husbandry, training, and public presentations of sea lions, harbor seals, and sea otters. Provides daily care for animals and facility. Trains specific behaviors according to the department's acceptable methods and guidelines for training. Provides public presentations of the animals. Interacts with the public in a professional and respectful manner. Relays all changes in method, techniques, and handling of animals.

TRAINER/SENIOR TRAINER

Department: Marine Mammals

Reports to: Assistant Curator of Marine Mammals

Hours: 40 hours, weekdays, weekends, holidays

Qualifications: Minimum high school graduate; B.A./B.S. in psychology or animal behavior preferred. Minimum one year experience handling/training marine mammals including sea otters. Scuba certification required.

Responsibilities: Responsible for the husbandry, training, and public presentations of sea lions, seals, and sea otters. Offers creative input for programs of animal care, public presentations, facility modifications and design. Acts as liaison for marine mammal and vet services departments. Demonstrates an understanding of basic training techniques and reinforcement schedules. Demonstrates an understanding of food fish ordering and purchasing process. Participates in basic outreach programs such as career day. Demonstrates a general knowledge of discovery life support systems.

PROGRAM DEVELOPMENT ASSISTANT

Department: Education

Reports to: Program Developer

Hours: 20 hours per week (flexible; potentially some evenings)

Qualifications: Experience with all or some of the following areas: museum education, marine biology, exhibit development, formative evaluation of exhibits or educational materials, graphic design, illustration, three-dimensional design and construction, and computer skills. Ability to work with school groups, families, and adult visitors to solicit ideas on exhibit prototypes. Strong office organization skills and ability to conduct phone and library research. Ability to handle multiple projects, work independently and with a team, work in high-paced environment, and meet deadlines. Ability to copy edit and proofread written materials.

Responsibilities: Conduct background research for the Georges Bank exhibit, including library and phone research, construction of prototypes, and involvement in the formation and evaluation of prototypes for Georges Bank. Will be responsible for the day-to-day aspects of office organization, including proofreading, sending out correspondence, ordering materials, filing, and other clerical tasks. Depending on the candidate's background, other responsibilities may include the physical design and fabrication of prototypes, photography, writing preliminary text, testing of prototypes, and graphic design and layout.

SUPERVISOR OF GALLERY AQUARISTS

Department: Fishes

Reports to: Curator of Fishes

Hours: Nine to five (35 hours per week)

Qualifications: Four-year college degree or equivalent with emphasis on biology or other science. Broad knowledge of the aquarium field, including animal husbandry, collection and exhibition of live specimens, and life support systems. Four years' experience as an aquarist. Strong supervisory skills. Ability to design and build life support systems and habitats. Strength and endurance to perform physical demands of the job. Must possess a nationally recognized scuba diver certification.

Responsibilities: Organizes and supervises the daily routines of gallery aquarists to ensure the proper appearance, operation, and husbandry of all live animal exhibits and support areas. Participates in the animal acquisition process to ensure that all exhibits contain a full complement of specimens. Reviews exhibits on a regular basis. Overseas the design, construction, maintenance, and installation of life support systems and exhibits. Develops and executes plans for improvements to existing exhibits and support areas. Conducts interviews and makes hiring recommendations for new aquarists. Conducts annual performance appraisals for aquarists.

SUPERVISOR OF SPECIAL EXHIBITS

Department: Fishes

Reports to: Curator of Fishes

Hours: Nine to five (35 hours per week)

Qualifications: Four-year college degree or its equivalent with emphasis on biology. Four years' experience as an aquarist. A broad knowledge of the aquarium field, including animal husbandry, collection and exhibition of live specimens and life support design, installation and operation. Strong supervisory skills. Strong communication, teamwork, and problem-solving skills. Nationally recognized scuba diver certification.

Responsibilities: Supervises the daily routines of special exhibit aquarists and program animal aquarists to ensure the proper appearance, operation, and husbandry of all live animal exhibits, laboratory animal programs, and support areas. Also responsible for research, development, and review of special exhibits. Oversees the design, installation, and construction phases of exhibits in conjunction with other departments. Oversees animal acquisition for special exhibits and education laboratory to ensure that all areas contain a full complement of specimens. Develops and executes plans for improvements to existing special exhibits. Conducts interviews and makes hiring recommendations for new aquarists. Conducts annual performance appraisals for special exhibit and education laboratory aquarists.

DIRECTOR OF PROGRAMS AND EXHIBITS

Department: Programs and Exhibits

Reports to: President

Hours: Nine to five, Monday through Friday

Qualifications: Minimum education required is a B.S./B.A. with extensive course work in aquatic sciences. Doctorate preferred. Three years of administrative and managerial experience in education, research, and exhibitry. Knowledge of information technology applications in education and exhibitry. Strong communication skills (written, verbal, interpersonal) and strategic planning, creative/coordination skills. Solid experience developing budgets and spreadsheets, cost controls, and staff supervision. Grant-writing skills a plus. Volunteer-coordination skill desired.

Responsibilities: Major leadership and liaison role in overseeing budgets and content goals of education, conservation, and research departments. Developing and supporting programs and exhibits with NEAq mission in view. Coordinating partnerships with schools, colleges, universities, research institutions, government agencies, and corporations.

VISITOR ASSISTANT

Department: Visitor Services

Reports to: Supervisor, Visitor Services

Hours: Monday through Friday

Qualifications: High school graduate comfortable in crowd situations. Excellent communication and interpersonal skills. Excellent attendance and punctuality essential. Cashier experience helpful.

Responsibilities: Provide first-class customer service. Assist public entry and exit process for mammal shows, main building, and special exhibits. Assist visitor services staff in various department functions.

FIRSTHAND ACCOUNTS

Steven Bailey, Curator of Fishes

Steven Bailey has been with the New England Aquarium since 1984. He received his bachelor's degree in zoology from Wilkes University in Wilkes-Barre, Pennsylvania, and completed substantial work toward a master's degree in ichthyology at Northeastern University in Boston. When a full-time job as an aquarist was offered to him at the aquarium, he jumped at the chance and has since moved up the ranks to his current position.

STEVEN BAILEY'S BACKGROUND

"When I was in graduate school, I was planning for a job that would pay me to go diving. It was as simple as that. I definitely had an animal thing going, and I had been diving since the sixties. My father, who is a forestry kind of guy, always outdoors, decided that my brother and I at a young age should know how to dive. I grew up in Pennsylvania but spent most of our summers diving at a lake in Maine. The perfect way to start.

"I spent four years in grad school, and they were incredibly busy years because I was trying to gain a lot of experience. I volunteered with the National Marine Fishery Service, and on a number of occasions I spent time as a professional collector, collecting specimens that were used for biomedical research. I had a great deal of diving experience, and back in the early eighties there weren't a lot of folks around applying for these positions who had that experience. I was working seven days a week and going to school and just generally maximizing every minute. I heard about the job because I was volunteering here while I was going to graduate school. I had a mentor here, too, who recommended me.

"I started as an aquarist. Over a thirteen-year period I moved up the ranks, or should I say I moved out of the best job in the building to the most aggravating job. I spent ten years as an aquarist, then I got promoted to senior aquarist and somehow, inexplicably, bypassed that last supervisor step and went from senior aquarist to my present position as curator of fish."

STEVEN BAILEY'S RESPONSIBILITIES

"As curator of fish, I am responsible for everything other than marine mammals. That's fish, invertebrates, reptiles, amphibians, birds, plants. My area involves the aquarium's two biggest exhibits, the Giant Ocean Tank, which is the centerpiece of the building—it's a 200,000-gallon Caribbean coral reef exhibit—and the penguin colony, which is at the base of the tank.

"I am responsible for twenty-four people. There are nineteen aquarists at different levels and four supervisors, the equivalent of assistant curators. I also supervise a curatorial associate who keeps track of everything from how much frozen food we are feeding fish to making sure all of our permits are up to date. She pitches in wherever she can, whether that's on a collecting trip or helping to haul a 500-pound turtle out of an exhibit for a blood sampling. "One of my duties is hiring. We can be incredibly selective about that. Every time there is a job opening advertised here we receive at least 200 resumes. We can be particular about the backgrounds that folks have. It must include diving, and it is up to them to make sure they have this training. They must also have a degree. Animal biology is preferred, but we also have people with environmental science or general biology degrees, too.

"People's work ethic is also very important; people who work hard to achieve a particular goal are very attractive to us. Sometimes you can see this on a resume. They want to be in contact with animals, so they'll do anything and everything to ensure that that happens, whether it's mucking out stalls, working for a vet, working in pet stores, running their own grooming businesses. There are a lot of things people can do to be close to animals. Being interested in fish is obviously a plus. Maybe someone has been a home hobbyist for years and can go on at length about the animals they've had in that time. Or maybe it is something they've developed more recently in life, as the result of a stimulating course they had in college. Some folks elect to do field experiences that are an epiphany to them. They manage to see something that they never thought of before and become quite enthralled with it.

"Primarily in this job I now deal with budget and personnel issues, or that's the way it seems. I am removed from the day-to-day hands-on work. If I had taken accounting courses and abnormal psychology, I would be much more prepared for this particular position than all the biology I studied.

"There are around eighty to ninety exhibits that fall under my group's control. Those range in size from the 200,000-gallon Caribbean Reef exhibit to a 50-gallon sea horse and pipe fish exhibit. Those exhibits need an incredible amount of scrutiny, from making sure the animals are nutritionally taken care of to the three W's, or aesthetics, of the exhibits—the windows, the walls, the water. They all have to be clean and aesthetically appealing, so that when folks come to visit us they are immediately assured that professionals are managing the animals. They spend money to visit here, and they should get a good return on their dollar. They are seeing the epitome of animal presentation, taking home a lot of good information and getting a bit of an education while they're here.

"Aquariums and zoos, in general, have evolved in many ways to where they are stewards of the animals in the wild. The long-term survival of these animals hinges upon the successes of zoos and aquariums in general. What I mean by this is there are many animals that are endangered or threatened or enjoy some sort of status of special concern, and we are breeding facilities, we are restocking facilities for animals that are ready to go back into the wild to reestablish a population. There is no substitute for seeing the real thing. We can get an important message across, and this is an admirable and worthwhile job.

"Conservation and research and animal breeding activities are all a big part of what zoos and aquaria are up to these days. We have an aquarist who spends a great deal of time in the Amazon each year. What he does is run an ecotourism operation where he has people paying to come on trips with him to assess biodiversity and explore the habitats of a number of these backwaters in the Amazon. The money generated from this is used to support Brazilian researchers who are doing things such as examining the ornamental fish industry. The most popular fish in the world, as far as the home aquarist goes, is a fish that comes out of the Rio Negro river system, a part of the Amazon River Basin. That animal is called the cardinal tetra. The cardinal tetra is single-handedly—or single-finnedly, I suppose—responsible for the well-being of maybe 40,000 to 50,000 people who live on that river. They are all in some way a part of that industry. Because they exact a living from that sustainable fishery and are not in the forest slash-and-burn agriculturing, or selling other animals skins or parts, it is one of the most intact areas of the basin.

"I preferred it when I was able to get out in the field instead of being parked in front of a computer screen all day and attending lots and lots of meetings. The positive aspects of this job are much different than what initially attracted me to the field. I don't get out and go collecting that often, but I do manage to get a fair amount of satisfaction and a sense of accomplishment from being involved in the design and exhibit-construction end of things. We, as a group—the husbandry folks, the design department, education, and research—get together to plot our course over the next few years.

"I am also married to someone who works here and is also an animal person, and life couldn't be better."

A WORD OF ADVICE

"It is a career for people who are very serious. There aren't that many opportunities and you have to be really dedicated to this pursuit. Most of the folks here have not been hired right out of college. They spent a good deal of time volunteering at this institution and picking up a lot of other related work experiences, expanding their horizons, becoming very much Renaissance people. The diversity of experiences that individuals can have are very important as far as making them attractive commodities when hiring time comes around. There are very few people here who were hired on their first go-around.

"This job requires that you have construction and tool skills. It demands you know your way around the literature or at least be able to find the information to answer a question or solve a problem. It requires an ability to be comfortable with routine and what can often become repetitive work.

"Being an aquatic chamber maid, which most everyone is, might sound like fun, but when you are cleaning and maintaining an animal's environment day after day, it can get very old for some people. For other people it's a Zen experience. They put it into perspective, they are able to be at peace with the incredible amount of responsibility they have for all of these animals.

"And not all of these animals have the excitement or energy that, say, a panda has or a killer whale. Those are animals that get a lot of attention from the public, but, nevertheless, an animal is an animal and whether you are talking about a minnow that is abundant five miles away from this institution or one of those more glamorous animals, such as the California sea otter, the bottom line is still the same. They depend on you, and you are responsible for their well-being."

VOLUNTEERING AT THE NEW ENGLAND AQUARIUM

"Volunteers are a very big part of the success of this institution. In the husbandry division we have volunteers donating something like 40,000 hours to us, so that's like twenty full-time positions. We also have summer and January term internships. The interns are supervised by fully trained aquarists and senior aquarists and they, in turn, are supervised by me.

"In addition to my staff, I have an incredible number of volunteers. The diving aquarists probably have twenty to twenty-five volunteers, and the gallery aquarists have about fifteen full-time volunteers. On a yearly basis we probably see twelve to eighteen interns."

Heather Urquhart, Senior Aquarist

Heather Urquhart is a diving aquarist in the Fishes Department at the New England Aquarium in Boston. She is a certified advanced scuba diver and has been working at the aquarium since 1989.

"I have always known that I wanted to work with animals. Early on I wasn't sure how, whether it would be veterinarian work or as a zookeeper. The opportunities I was aware of then for working with animals were limited. After I saw Jacques Cousteau, I knew I wanted to work with marine animals. I've always been an ocean buff; I grew up at the ocean. When I was a kid, I was always the one without a suntan. I always had my mask and snorkel on.

"I got a B.S. degree in biology with a concentration in marine biology and a chemistry minor at Salem State College in 1985. Before I got my job here, I thought for sure I'd be going on for a master's, but once you get involved with your work doing something that you love, it's hard to break away to go back to school.

"Growing up in this area, I was always aware of the aquarium and what was going on. When I started school in Salem, which is very close to the city, I found out through friends at school about the aquarium's volunteer opportunities. While I was still in college, I volunteered here for six months, two days a week in 1984, coincidentally in the area in which I am now working, with the penguins. Also at the time we had river otters that we took care of. I was able to group all my classes on Mondays, Wednesdays, and Fridays, so I could volunteer on Tuesdays and Thursdays.

"Once I graduated in 1985, I had a couple of other jobs—I worked with an environmental consulting firm for six months and did some quality control work with seafood—but was constantly applying whenever a position came open here. I'd scan the newspapers and then send my resume in. It took a little while, but finally they brought me in for an interview, and based on the good recommendations I had received as a volunteer and my interview I got hired. That was in 1989 and I've been here ever since. I started as an aquarist-in-training, then to aquarist, then to my current title, senior aquarist. I am in the Fishes Department. Even though I work with the penguins, they are classified under the fish department."

HEATHER URQUHART'S RESPONSIBILITIES

"I take care of both the Giant Ocean Tank and the penguin colony. I dive into the tank up to five times a day in order to feed and examine and check on the health of the fish as well as clean and maintain the exhibit. We have five dives going a day, so if we have enough people in we'll rotate, so sometimes we don't have to go in every day.

"The penguin exhibit has a 150,000-gallon tank and we need seven staff people to maintain both exhibits, plus we have volunteers to help us seven days a week. We have forty-seven penguins right now. We don't have to dive in the penguin exhibit, but we do have to put on a wet suit to get in there. We are in fifty-five degree water up to our chest. There are days you just don't feel like getting wet, but you just grin and bear it. If one of us is ill with a bad cold or the flu, then we try to accommodate each other, but even then I've gone in. There was no choice. The fish have to be fed.

"It's a very physical job and it's not for everyone. Not only because you're in the water, but just the nature of putting on dive equipment and chugging down the hall to get into the tank, then pulling yourself out. Then, there's going up and down four flights of stairs in order to get to the penguin exhibit with fifteen pounds of fish in a bucket in each hand. There is an elevator, but it's a big freight elevator, and by the time you get yourself in there and down, it's just easier to take the stairs. Besides that you need a key to open the elevator, and when you're in a wet suit in saltwater, you don't want to be carrying around metal keys. They corrode.

"Lately my concentration has been with the penguins more. We don't do any training with the penguins, we want people to see them as they would be in the wild. We do have some penguins, though, that have been partially hand-raised, and they tend to be more accustomed to human interaction. These penguins we can take out and do what we call an animal interview. They are put in an enclosure outside of the exhibit where visitors, without touching the animal, can still get an up-close and personal look. Some of our staff members will speak about the animal and give a presentation. Although they aren't trained per se, these animals don't mind being in the spotlight. It's a joy to work with them.

"I enjoy the animal interactions the most, it's some of the best medicine going. No matter what kind of aggravating day you might be having, when you are working with the animals, it all seems not to matter so much.

"I've been here for quite a while and I've hand-raised a lot of little penguins, and that's a wonderful experience—to be there from the egg to the adult stage. They imprint on you and they know my voice and will come to me. We have them all banded, but I can recognize who's who. Once the hand-raised penguins mature a little and become interested in a mate, they tend to ignore us more. We are no longer as interesting to them.

"We keep a genealogy on all our penguins and we keep food records and medical records and records of molting patterns. We also monitor their mating patterns to prevent inbreeding. If we notice two that would make a bad pair, we separate them and encourage each of them to breed with a penguin that would be a better match. In the wild you don't have that problem, but here we have to be careful. And with this particular species we have to be careful because their numbers are so vulnerable in the wild right now.

"In addition to maintaining the exhibit, I've been lucky enough to form a conservation program surrounding our penguins. We house two species of penguins, rock hopper and the African penguin. The African penguins are on the verge of becoming an endangered species in the wild. Through the help of the aquarium, we've been able to set up a fund and generate monies here through a penny-smasher machine. It costs 51 cents—we keep the 50 cents and the penny goes under a barrel that has the imprint of an African penguin on it. The penny gets smooshed with the logo on it and the kids get a souvenir. In the past two years I've been to South Africa twice and intend to go again soon. We link up with conservation organizations there and join them on their conservation and research work, trying to contribute as much as we can, as well as bringing back the most factual data to the States to educate people about the penguins' plight. We are also educating ourselves. We want to be more than talking heads who have never been in the field. We also contribute to penguin rehabilitation organizations that are helping oiled penguins in South Africa. We have great hopes for the future—we are really moving and shaking with this thing. The past two years have been wonderful, a real windfall for me.

"We do a lot of local travel up and down the East Coast for collecting fish and invertebrates for our exhibits. We also run a collecting trip twice a year down to the Bahamas to collect for our Caribbean Reef exhibit. But we don't have to collect that much because we are pretty good at maintaining the exhibit.

"We have sharks in our Caribbean exhibit that we dive with, but they probably are what I worry about least in there. They are docile and they don't pay much attention to us. I think people have a lot of misconceptions about sharks. People aren't on a shark's menu, and a lot of times attacks are the result of mistaken identity. In our tank we have some fish that are only about an inch or an inch and a half long, yet they are much more aggressive than any shark. Little damsel fish protecting their nests will come right out at you, for example. I've been bitten by damsel fish on numerous occasions. We get our share of bites, not only from the fish, but from the penguins, too. They aren't trying to be mean, but you're down there feeding them and handling them, and they aren't tame animals. Most of the time it's our own mistake. You're feeding a little piece of shrimp to a fish and they miss the shrimp and get your finger. They don't take your finger off, but you get little nips and bites. Nothing serious. Probably the Stranding Department has to worry more getting bitten by a seal they are trying to rescue who is sick."

A WORD OF ADVICE

"Volunteer, volunteer, volunteer. That's the best bet. Not only will the people who work at the institution get to know your work, but you'll get an idea of what you'd be getting into, too.

"The glamorous part is that you get to work with a lot of cute baby animals. But the nonglamorous part is all that other stuff of being in a wet suit all day long in cold water and smelling like fish by the end of the day. Ninety percent of working with animals is cleaning up after them. It's not for everyone.

"But if it is for you, then volunteering is the way to go. The vast majority of the people working here formerly volunteered here. We do pull from within our ranks.

"Also, make sure you go to school, but don't specialize too much early on. For the type of job I have, you'd need to have a biology or zoology degree, one of these general topics. Then if you get to do some volunteer work, you can see more clearly what area to focus on. You might decide you want to work in a lab or in education."

Scott Dowd, Senior Aquarist

Scott Dowd is a gallery aquarist in the Fishes Department at the New England Aquarium in Boston. He started as a temporary aquarist in 1987, then was promoted to an aquarist-in-training, then a trained aquarist, and finally to his current position as senior aquarist.

SCOTT DOWD'S BACKGROUND

"When I was young there was a pond behind my parent's house, and I spent all of my time there. Then I started bringing things home from the pond. Frogs, salamanders, turtles, fish. I had extremely tolerant parents, but my mother was very uncomfortable with snakes. I interpreted that to mean if she *knew* I had snakes. So my job was to keep her from finding out about the snakes. I'd get calls to come home from school now and then to catch the stray snake in the living room.

"I went to college because I wanted a job in this field, but I was a terrible student. I started volunteering at the aquarium in 1985 while I was a student, but I had already worked in the field. In fact, I've never done anything but take care of fish. I kept a lot of tropical fish, and at eight years old I had a great rapport with the pet store. I'd shop at flea markets and was able to build a pretty impressive fish room. Later, I worked in pet shops, and I had a little business that I started taking care of people's fish tanks in their homes and offices.

"In 1987, because I was doing so poorly in school, I got a letter from the college saying basically that I was out. A week later I got offered a full-time job at the aquarium. I had been under the impression that I had to finish school to get a job here, but I had been volunteering a lot, putting in a lot of extra time and doing some special projects on my own. I didn't feel particularly that I was contributing. I thought the aquarium was just indulging me. But I guess I had made a bit of a name for myself, and when someone left the aquarium, they approached me and asked if I wanted to work there full-time. I thought everything was going wrong because of my college experience, but in the end it all made sense. The reason I did so poorly in school was because I spent so much time with fish. But all that time I spent with fish led to my developing the professional experience that enabled me to get my job. I didn't get the classical education, but I followed my heart."

SCOTT DOWD'S RESPONSIBILITIES

"My primary area of responsibility is the freshwater gallery. I maintain the health of the animals, the appearance of the display, and the life support systems, the holding and quarantine areas.

"The official name of my gallery is the Rivers of the Americas gallery. It is a comparison between North American and South American river systems, holding, among other things, arawana, pacu, piranha, cichlids, tetras, and catfish.

"We have to be extremely independent in this position and set our own priorities, but at the same time we have to work in a tight team situation. The people attracted to this field are passionate about it. And when you get people's emotions involved, it sometimes makes it challenging to work together. People are so personally driven and committed to our conservation goals but they have their own ideas how to do things, so teamwork and compromise are essential. It's an intense job. And it isn't the highest paying job. People are doing this because of their personal motivation.

"In the morning I do a procedure called check in. I have a lot of sophisticated life support systems. I take an hour before the public comes in and view my exhibits to make sure the water looks good and is circulating and the lights are working. But the most important thing I do at this time is look at the fish. When you've been working with fish for a long time, you can tell at a glance if something's wrong. Their color patterns, their behavior, their posture— are all clues. It could be something subtle, maybe a fish needs a better hiding place or more fish of the same species in the exhibit. Or it could be something blatant, a fish has been injured or come down with a disease. Medical issues are dealt with by our vet services department. We work together to form a diagnosis and a treatment.

"After I check the exhibits, I come in back and look at every single valve and I feel every single plug and I check every detail to make sure nothing has gone wrong overnight. Then I manually take temperatures of all the exhibit. Every exhibit and every holding tank has a chart. I put the thermometer in the water and record it on the chart.

"After that I feed the fish. Because the fish we have are very diverse, their diets, too, are diverse. I also maintain the exhibits. I have to keep the glass and the background clean. I have two large exhibits that I have to go into to scrub algae. For that I put on a wet suit and wade into the tanks. Diving isn't part of my job. It is required, though, to be a certified diver. I became certified through a private dive shop.

"Since we are a thirty-year-old place and aquarium science is rapidly evolving, we don't have to look far to find something that needs to be brought up to speed. We try to do it on a priority basis. If something is really old or outdated or needs servicing, we address that situation first. We are nonprofit, so resources are limited and we can't do everything we'd like to do. But though we might be limited by resources, we aren't limited by enthusiasm or time. We can often put in seven days and seven nights a week.

"I officially work Tuesday through Saturday, but sometimes I've gone six-month stretches without taking a day off. I often find myself running to catch the last train home after midnight. And sometimes I'll spend the night here.

"The downsides are that I'll never get rich. I've been here ten years and am now earning about $30,000. It's not poverty level, but in Boston, it's not great either. And the time I put in eats into my personal life.

"But I love being an aquarist and taking care of fish. It's what I do. I think the world is in severe crisis with the environmental issues going on and it's very rewarding to know that you are committing yourself to an institution that has a goal of changing that."

A WORD OF ADVICE

"I think that the door I came through is closed now. In fact, I couldn't get the job I have now if I were applying off the street. The requirement now is that you must have a degree.

"Since this job is so demanding and requires so much compromise and the opportunities are so diverse, people have to make sure they are pursuing something they are genuinely interested in."

Jenny Montague, Assistant Curator/Animal Trainer

Jenny Montague is assistant curator in the Marine Mammals Department at the New England Aquarium. Her position is equivalent to the supervisor job title in the Fishes Department. She has been with the aquarium since 1988.

JENNY MONTAGUE'S BACKGROUND

"I started working at Marine World/Africa USA in Vallejo, California, a marine mammal zoo combination, as a landscaper while I was still in high school. It was an odd existence for a while. I was desperately trying to get into marine mammals, so I'd be at Marine World at five in the morning to do landscaping, then I had to go to school, and afterward I'd come back and work until dark.

"I did some community college but I got hired as an assistant trainer in the marine mammals department at Marine World right out of high school. That was 1981. I stayed there for eight years and left there as a senior trainer/show manager. I came to Boston right after that as supervisor of marine mammals. The woman who is curator here had worked briefly at Marine World on a research project, so we got to know each other. When the supervisor opening came up, she called me and I said yes pretty quickly. I was ready for a change. As much as I liked Marine World, I felt I had probably gone as far as I could go in the hierarchy. I was interviewed over the phone and our history together clinched the deal."

JENNY MONTAGUE'S RESPONSIBILITIES

"I am basically a trainer who has worked her way up through the ranks to an assistant curator position. I do more paperwork than I'd like to, but my basic job right now is to oversee the training and health of the animals. I supervise eight staff people. They range from assistant trainer to senior trainer.

"We work with the colony or resident marine mammals, which include Atlantic harbor seals, California sea lions, and California sea otters. We are responsible for the training, the care, and the presentation to the public of these mammals. We are located next door to the aquarium on the floating barge, what they call the Barge Discovery. It's an indoor show because of the weather we have in Boston. There are between four and seven shows daily, divided up amongst our staff. Sometimes three or four staff members are involved in the presentation if we're working with more than one animal. I personally do about eight or ten shows a week."

JENNY'S ROLE AS ANIMAL TRAINER

"We're interested in portraying to the public what the animals' background is, what their natural history is, and also some of the conservation issues that surround them. We do that in what we hope is a fun and educational way. When people can get close to live animals it makes an incredible impression on them. All different levels of trainers participate, from the assistant trainers to assistant curators. We get out there with the animals and talk to the audience about the different animal behaviors, explaining how they are able to do what they do. We do a little about the physiology and the biology of the animals and also about the training techniques we use. We'll do a demonstration of some of the medical behaviors we have, such as brushing the animals' teeth. They are all trained to sit or lie still and allow a stethoscope to be put on them. They are trained to lie still for x-rays. They open their mouths to let the veterinarians look down their throat. They'll sit still for an eye exam.

"The training is for the medical care of the animals, but it's also for mental stimulation. We find that, like anyone, if they are stimulated mentally and physically, they are much happier and healthier animals than if they are just left alone. We feel that training is a very important part of animal management in zoos and aquariums.

"During the presentations, we encourage audience members to participate. We ask them if they can give suggestions as to what we can do as individuals to keep the ocean a safer place for the animals. And anybody that has an interesting idea gets to come down and meet the sea lion. They get to pat him and get a kiss.

"When we are doing training, we keep records of all the advances the animals make and what new steps they've accomplished. Each individual animal has a primary trainer. I happen to be primary trainer right now for Ballou, a six-year-old male California sea lion. There are usually two primary trainers for each animal, so every day can be covered. We are basically responsible for regularly weighing the animals, looking at their diet, and making sure they are getting the proper amount of food. All of the fish we feed them is sent out for analysis, so we know exactly how many calories and how many grams of fat are in each kind of fish. We run that through a formula and calculate the right amount based on the animal's age and weight.

"The two primary trainers work as a team and are responsible for deciding what the animal is going to learn, who of the two will train it, and what methods we'll use.

"Each animal has its own personality. Some animals you can work on a particular behavior with for half an hour and do several repeats, and then they make a step. We have one sea lion that if we repeat things over and over and lead him slowly through little steps, he'll never forget what you've taught him. Another one, Guthrie, gets bored very easily, and he starts to add in his own special flair. We spend more time retraining him than training him, to get rid of all his extraneous stuff. But he's a howl, one of the most fun sea lions to work with.

"How many hours you spend on something depends a lot on the animals and how much they are enjoying it and want to work with you. Tyler, a thirteen-year-old sea lion, isn't too crazy about having his teeth touched, so we'll only do that once or twice at a time. But he does like the other medical behaviors. He loves to lie around for x-rays, he likes the vets to touch him, but you really have to go slow with his mouth.

"We also do show behaviors, high jumps and hitting a ball, for example. One we're working on now is a gallop, which shows the audience how quickly the sea lions can run on land. We work the sea lions in conjunction with our harbor seals sometimes, and there is a major difference in speed between the two. The sea lions are much faster. The seals slug along on their bellies; they're not the most graceful creatures on land. A lot of this might seem circusy, but we are actually just trying to demonstrate the natural behavior of the animal. They're taught to do porpoising, for example, which is a natural behavior. What we teach them is to do it on command.

"We also train for research behaviors. Recently we started a hearing study, and we're at the beginning stages of teaching the animals to allow us to put headphones on them. At the same time, they're being taught to respond to a sound cue. We also taught a sea lion to distinguish between the size of two objects and choose the larger one."

ANIMAL TRAINING METHODS

"We use three different training methods. Operant conditioning is the one most widely used. You break a behavior into small steps and you lead the animal through the steps, providing reinforcement along the way.

"Another method is called innovative. Where operant conditioning is based on repetition, with innovative we are asking the animals to create something new. After they have a solid operant conditioning understanding, we give them an arbitrary signal, which is crossing our arms across our chest. They have no idea what it means, but they might confuse it with a signal they do know and will offer a behavior. At the beginning we would reward the old behavior, but then we'll only reward every new behavior. We use a variety of reinforcers, like fish, or some of the animals like to be scratched and rubbed down. You spend a lot of time trying to find what the animals enjoy. Some like particular toys, others like things like ice cubes. So, for example, after the signal, they might give a salute. We'll reward it and then, because they are familiar with operant conditioning, they figure that if they do it again, they'll be rewarded again. But the next time we don't reinforce the salute. You can get a curious look from them at that point. We'll give the signal again, and if the salute doesn't work yet again, they'll start to offer something else, whether it's a look in another direction or moving their whiskers forward in a curious questioning look. All of those little subtle movements are rewarded, and they start coming up with some pretty wild things. The purpose of this is to stimulate their creativity. It allows them to do things they like to do and it keeps them thinking. It also gives the training staff some ideas. A lot of times they'll come up with things we wouldn't have thought of. Our sea lion, Zack, used to carry some rings around on his flippers and slap them at the same time. He had all his flippers going and then he'd roll over. It was this amazing little dance that he did.

"The third method is called mimicry training. We ask the animals to focus on us and copy what we do. We got the idea for this because they already did mimic us to some extent. Some of the things they'll mimic is turning around in a circle or hopping up or opening a mouth or making a sound. It's really fun, and the benefit of that is it gives them a whole different focus. They have to watch our whole bodies completely, instead of just the usual hand gestures."

THE UPSIDES AND DOWNSIDES

"One of the nicest things about the job is that you never run out of ideas and you're able to try them out. It's always different every day.

"On the downside, the hours are inconsistent and you can't rely on a nine-to-five day. Most of our staff work four ten-hour days. We are open seven days a week. Something always comes up, though, which prevents you from a regular schedule, but then, on the other hand, that might be a good thing."

A WORD OF ADVICE

"My advice would be to find any one of the schools that work with animal behavior. The interesting part of this job is that there are different academic subjects that can help you, such as psychology, animal behavior, and some zoology. Marine biology, however, is not a direct lead to the training field. It's a misconception a lot of people have. When I was in school, it was pretty difficult finding people who were doing animal behavior work. It was happening but it wasn't as accessible as it is today. It wasn't really considered a career path, and if you wanted to work with animal behavior, you did training with pigeons and rats. There are formal training schools now. One is EATM, Exotic Animal Training and Management, in Moorpark, California. [See Appendix A.] There is also a strong program at the University of California in Santa Cruz. IMATA, the International Marine Animal Trainers Association, can provide a list of all the training programs. [See Appendix A.]

"I also strongly suggest that people volunteer. A lot of the time folks come and see animal shows and think that's all there is to it. But it isn't. We're up to our elbows in sinks full of dead fish all the time. We're running around in rubber boots all the time and you do get damp. There's a lot more to it than the time on the stage. As a volunteer, you'd get a sense of all that.

"It is also important to visit different institutions. Everyone has a different style."

CHAPTER 8

EDUCATION AND
PUBLIC RELATIONS

One of the most vital roles of zoos and aquariums is public education. With more than 115 million people visiting zoos and aquariums each year, it is a marvelous opportunity to foster positive attitudes toward wildlife. In recent years these facilities have become informal education centers that allow visitors to learn and experience at their own pace.

Almost all zoos and aquariums provide some sort of educational programming for the public. Educators and program developers design classes, workshops, lectures, and tours and often offer outreach programs to the schools or local community in which they are located.

Even though we are flooded with information through television, movies, videos, and books, nothing can replace the full impact of seeing living animals face to face. Zoos and aquariums serve their communities by supplying interesting facts and, in some cases, hands-on experiences in a friendly, family-based setting. Their public education goals are to encourage visitors to become part of the conservation solution by enhancing their awareness and appreciation of wildlife.

EDUCATION METHODS

The methods used are as varied as the makeup of the visitors. Through interaction with zookeepers, trained docents, volunteers, and education staff members, information is conveyed with publications, graphics, and naturally designed exhibits. And, of course, nothing carries as much weight as the chance to observe animal behavior firsthand.

THE AUDIENCES EDUCATORS REACH

With more than eight million students participating in field trips to zoos and aquariums each year, it is the perfect opportunity for classroom teachers and staff educators to put their heads together and design curricula to meet the needs of specific classes.

Zoo educational services reach beyond the confines of the specific facility. Educators go into the community through outreach programs, visiting hospitals, nursing homes, and community centers. They also bring exhibits and information directly into the schools, both public and private.

Zoos and aquariums also provide training for classroom teachers. AZA zoo and aquarium educators reach more than 25,000 teachers a year through in-service training courses. Topics are varied and cover such issues as endangered species, threatened habitats, and educational methodologies for field trips.

REQUIREMENTS FOR EDUCATORS

Educators usually possess a teaching certificate or have had teaching experience before they join a zoo or aquarium staff. They arrange programs for the public, explain the exhibits, conduct classes, and often do outreach work with local schools and other community organizations.

Tour guides, or docents, as they are often called, usually fall under the realm of the education department. Many tour guides work on a volunteer basis, are knowledgeable about certain exhibits, and have excellent speaking skills.

Most museums produce in-house publications—such as brochures, pamphlets, newsletters, catalogs, books, and other promotional materials. Editors and writers usually have a college degree and possess strong editorial skills.

SALARIES FOR EDUCATORS

As in any setting, salaries for zoo and aquarium educators are far from glamorous. The average is in the high twenties. The top educator staff member or director could earn approximately $40,000 a year.

PUBLIC RELATIONS

Within zoos and aquariums a variety of personnel work together to make known the services the facility has to offer. Marketing personnel work on advertising campaigns and organize activities to increase public awareness of the institution.

Public relations (PR) professionals also help promote the facility and its mission as well as its programs via the media.

Special events staff develop and carry out activities to attract visitors to the institution throughout the year.

Other duties for all these related job titles include writing press releases and advertising copy for promotional literature.

SALARIES WITHIN PUBLIC RELATIONS

The salaries for marketing and PR specialists run closely to those earned by education staff. Salaries can begin in the high teens and run more than $40,000 a year, with an average annual income of approximately $33,000.

CLOSE-UP: METROZOO, MIAMI

Metrozoo is located on 740 acres in south Miami and is home to more than 900 live specimens of mammals, reptiles, and birds. Regarded as an impressive zoo—a showplace, by other top-notch facilities around the country—in the past few years Metrozoo has more than proved itself worthy of the compliments. In 1992 Hurricane Andrew chose Metrozoo like an arrow homing in on a target's bull's-eye. Every facility and every exhibit was damaged or completely destroyed. Acres of Everglades forest and mangrove swamps were flattened, and trees bent or ripped out at their roots. The winds were so fierce, they yanked the monorail tracks off their steel supports and hurled trailers beyond fences into the animal exhibits.

The morning after the storm every employee reported in, ready to get to work, even those who had lost their own homes to Andrew's wrath. The devastation that greeted them was offset by something nothing less than miraculous. With the exception of 135 dead or missing birds from the destroyed aviary, only five other mammals were found dead. The workers also found another miracle. A small antelope had given birth during the storm; her newborn (appropriately named Andrew) was discovered in a zoo moat!

Although the animals had survived, many had scattered, and the trauma they had endured was evident. Over time many returned on their own to the only home they knew; one pheasant was even rescued from the Florida Turnpike.

The three hours of storm damage Andrew produced took four years to rebuild. All the exhibits, except for the aviary, which is still waiting for funding to come through, are open now. The weeks and months and years the staff spent clearing the debris, caring for the animals, and rebuilding the exhibits has made them an incredibly cohesive team. New employees to Metrozoo will find it a special environment in which to work.

Salaries at Metrozoo

Metrozoo is a county-run facility that provides competitive salaries and excellent benefits. Entry-level workers start at about $16,000 to $17,000 a year. Senior keepers earn approximately $25,000 (see Chapter 2 for more zookeeping information), and assistant curators can expect $30,000 to $35,000. Communications director Ron Magill (profiled below), with many years of service now makes $55,000 a year. Someone new to his particular job would start out in the $35,000 to $38,000 range.

Animal-Related Positions at Metrozoo

Metrozoo claims about sixty positions that are directly animal related. Ron Magill admits that they are probably understaffed. He says, "One of the greatest compliments I could give Metrozoo is that it does a tremendous amount with very little available to it as far as staffing goes."

Job titles found at Metrozoo are similar to those in other facilities. They include keepers, curators, zoological supervisors (field supervisors positions below the assistant curator level), educators, and a veterinarian and vet tech. (See Chapter 5 for Metrozoo veterinarian and vet tech firsthand accounts.)

Education Programs at Metrozoo

The education department at Metrozoo designs programs that offer hands-on experience to participants. They include offering school field trips, the Zoofari Summer Camp, minizoo camps, and a weekend adventure series.

Metrozoo's education department also participates in helping young people explore the possibilities of future zoo-related careers. Students get a behind-the-scenes look at exhibits and a chance to talk with the professionals who work there. Contact the education department for more information. Their address is:

Miami Metrozoo
12400 SW 152nd Street
Miami, FL 33177

FIRSTHAND ACCOUNT

Ron Magill, Zoo Communications Director

Ron Magill has been with Metrozoo in Miami since 1980. He started as a zookeeper and moved his way up through the ranks. As the zoo spokesperson, he has made numerous appearances on television programs such as the *David Letterman Show, Good Morning America, The Today Show,* and *CNN.*

RON MAGILL'S BACKGROUND

"What got me hooked on this business was as a small child watching shows like *Wild Kingdom* or *National Geographic.* My hero as a boy was Jim Fowler, the host of *Wild Kingdom.* Within the last five years, I have been fortunate enough to not only meet him, but he's been at my house and we've worked on international projects together. For me I still feel like I am a lucky little boy who has had his dreams answered.

"I was a zoology major at the University of Florida. I had received an associate's degree and was working toward a bachelor's. I had heard that a big new zoo was being built in Miami, so I had put in my application. I wanted to be involved from the ground floor. In my senior year I received a phone call that there was a zookeeper opening at Metrozoo. I left college to take the job. In college I had also worked at the Florida State Museum in the herpetology section (reptiles and amphibians), and I had done a lot of research work in Mexico through National Science Foundation grants. I also took a job during my college breaks working at the Miami Serpentarium with Bill Haast. He is one of the top people in the field. I learned a lot about management and handling of these reptiles from him, and so I had a lot of experience to offer.

"You learn that if you want to work with wildlife, you have to take the opportunity when it knocks. I remember when I left college my parents were somewhat disappointed that I wasn't finishing my degree, but I understood then that this was a good job, and if you had a chance to get it, to get in the door, you had to take it. In hindsight I made the right decision. I was able to elevate myself through the ranks, and now I believe I have the best job in the world.

"I started here in 1980 as a zookeeper and went up the ranks to lead zookeeper, senior zookeeper, and then assistant curator in charge of first shows and public demonstrations, then quarantine, and finally the reptile department.

"As a curator I was responsible for managing certain elements of the collection. I managed the reptile collection, setting up breeding situations and pairing the animals. I designed exhibits and helped to decide the diets with the veterinarians. I supervised the zookeepers who managed the direct day-to-day care of the animals, and I communicated a great deal with other curatorial staff and with other zoos around the country." (For more information about curatorial positions see Chapter 3.)

RON MAGILL'S JOB DESCRIPTION

"Now I am the zoo spokesperson. I do a lot of the television programs, a lot of the public appearances and speaking engagements. I act as a liaison with the media and also write press releases. My job is similar to what Jack Hannah does at the Columbus Zoo and Joan Embery did at the San Diego Zoo.

"Of all the positions I have held at Metrozoo, this is the best one. Each one has pluses, though. In this job I don't have as much exposure in the field that I used to have, but the beauty is that I still get a lot of hands-on contact because when I do these programs I get to handle the animals.

"What I enjoy the most is the contact with the public, especially with children. The kids are my greatest inspiration, and they have a real love for animals. Not to sound too much like a cliché, but children really are our future, and if we can show this generation how important our wildlife is then we are doing a great job.

"My job is different every day. I've been here seventeen-plus years and I am still amazed at how it can still be so exciting. I don't have to wear a suit and a tie and sit behind a desk or go into any kind of methodical assembly line type of work. I have been able to travel around the world and to see things that as a small boy I only dreamed of.

"When I first went to Africa, for example, on a familiarization trip so I could lead tours and promote the area, I looked out over the Serengeti and saw nothing but wildlife and nature. It was mind-boggling. I got tears in my eyes. This job has provided me with such incredible privileges.

"I do programs and slide presentations, and because I've been there I can relay the excitement I have about the place. I've also been to the Galapagos Islands, and now I am working on a project in Panama to save the harpy eagle. It is the national bird of Panama and highly endangered now. When I first started, very few people in Panama even knew what a harpy eagle was. I set up a program that is analogous to what we did in the United States with the bald eagle in the seventies and it has been so successful. I've received letters from President Clinton, the president of Panama, and the mayor of Panama. It has turned into a real campaign, not just to save the harpy eagle but to save the tropical rain forests in Panama.

"There are always downsides, of course. Here it is that you are always facing budget crises. You are always trying to get more for less, and it can be very frustrating. Today the discretionary dollar is very difficult to obtain and zoos struggle. If you don't get the attendance you need to bring in the dollar, some of the projects you're working on and some of the goals you have set might suffer. You always try to build new exhibits and improve exhibits and provide better visitor amenities and to bring new state-of-the-art programs and projects to the zoo. We love to be more involved with research with other countries.

"If I didn't have to pay bills, I wouldn't even want to take money for my job. For me it is such a privilege."

A WORD OF ADVICE

"If you get a job offer, take it. When I interview people here for jobs at the zoo, I put a great deal more weight on actual experience with exotic animals than on education. It is preferable, of course, to have both, but if it's one or the other, and someone has already proven himself or herself in the field with these exotic animals, I tend to think that's more important. I've seen many students come out of school with a straight A average, model students in every way, but they have a difficult time applying that knowledge to the field.

"You should try to get experience at some of the smaller attractions. Here in Florida we have a lot of wildlife rehabilitation facilities, places like Monkey Jungle and Parrot Jungle. There they don't require a great deal of experience because the pay is not substantial. They can say, "we won't pay you much but we will give you a chance to get that experience." And I try to tell people, listen when you're young, money is not as important as you think it is. Get the experience. That experience will pay off as you get older and develop your career."

CHAPTER 9

VOLUNTEERING IN ZOOS AND AQUARIUMS

Although formal, academic training is vital to your resume, hands-on experience is of equal importance. Not only does it provide a host of significant skills that will help you get your foot in the door for a paid position, it also allows the career explorer to make an informed decision about the suitability of zoo or aquarium work. A person who starts with a term of volunteer work, even before beginning a college program, will have a better idea of what career options zoos have to offer and whether these options are right for him or her.

SETTINGS FOR VOLUNTEERS

Many zoos and aquariums rely heavily on volunteer energy and can place volunteers in almost every department, from tour guide and gift shop sales to assisting curators, tank divers, and exhibit designers.

GETTING STARTED

The easiest way to volunteer your time is to call a zoo and ask to speak to the volunteer coordinator. He or she will work with you to match your interests with the zoo's needs.

Volunteer programs are usually flexible about the number of hours and days per week they expect from their volunteers.

INTERNSHIPS

In addition, many zoos and aquariums have their own internship programs that are offered to full-time students as well as recent graduates. You can check with your university department first to see what arrangements they traditionally make. If the burden is on you to arrange an internship, either during your academic program or after you've graduated, contact the zoo's internship coordinator. If the zoo has no formal internship program, talk first to a zoo staff member to determine where there might be a need. Then you can write a proposal incorporating your interests in a department where help will be appreciated.

Internships can be either paid or unpaid and are usually a more formal arrangement than volunteering. The number of hours and weeks will be structured, and the intern might be expected to complete a specific project during his or her time there. Often college credit can be given.

Later, when it comes time to job hunt, a successful internship or stint of volunteer work can open the door at the training institution or at other zoos. In addition, volunteering is often a way to learn of permanent positions. After all, if you are right there on the spot and a position opens up, you'll be one of the first to know. Most employers would hire someone they already have worked with than some unknown entity out of the blue. If you have proven yourself through your volunteer work, you come to the job interview with a built-in advantage.

FIRSTHAND ACCOUNTS

Charles Leblanc, Volunteer

Charles LeBlanc is Senior Zoo Corps Officer in the Department of Education at the Audubon Zoological Garden in New Orleans. He is a high school student who has been volunteering his time since 1995.

Getting started is simple. "I sent in an application and they accepted me," Charles explains. "I want to become a vet later in life, and I want to learn more about animals while learning other skills such as speaking in public and doing presentations. This job is perfect for that. I also went to the Teton Science School for two weeks to learn about nature, and I attended the Texas A&M Leadership Camp.

"I absolutely love what I do. It appeals to me in almost every way. As a volunteer, I have a very relaxed day; it is very interesting and I'm never bored. I teach visitors about the animals; it helps them realize that they can make a difference. I want people to know that they can help the endangered species list grow shorter.

"Also, for me, learning about each animal both generally and personally is like a never-ending soap opera. Each animal has his or her own unique way of acting.

"My job involves collecting the available information in the park and taking it a step beyond. Some of the smaller animals I can take out and actually let people touch while they ask questions.

"My hours, of course, vary. I can work whenever I want. The atmosphere is wonderful. Most of the keepers are happy to be around each other, and there is virtually no friction between co-workers.

"With this job, I feel as if I'm giving something to the community. It is community money, after all, that helps to keep the research going so we can protect our endangered animals. I also love to teach our visitors. The only downside to my job is when it rains or when I run into a difficult visitor who just doesn't want to follow the rules."

Karyn Myers, Volunteer

Karyn Myers is a paid legal secretary/paralegal who volunteers her time in the aviculture department at the Aquarium of the Americas in New Orleans. With a career as a vet planned, she is currently enrolled at the University of New Orleans working toward a bachelor of science degree. After that, it will be on to veterinary school. Karyn also has prior experience working for the Grosse Pointe Animal Clinic in Michigan. She has been involved in this field since 1988.

GETTING STARTED

"I have always liked animals, even more than most people," Karyn explains. "It all started when I was babysitting and the child's guinea pig got sick. We went to the clinic, and the doctor later approached me about a position he had available working as a receptionist/kennel help. I accepted the job, and by the time I left I was assisting in surgery.

"I moved to New Orleans in April of 1993. I had already visited the aquarium three times before I discovered that they had a volunteer program. I enrolled at the end of the summer and passed all their criteria, becoming a naturalist volunteer. This position required working on the floor directly with the public, providing information about the animals as well as the facility.

"Soon after, I started working at functions in the evening and assisting with sleep-overs with families and boy and girl scout troops.

"Approximately two years later, I approached the curator of birds and inquired about becoming an aviculture volunteer. I was accepted and transferred to the aviculture department where I now work with macaws, parrots, penguins, and many small free-flying birds. I still assist with the naturalist volunteer work occasionally, as well as the parties and sleep-overs. I have also had the opportunity to help the saltwater and freshwater departments care for their exhibits and animals."

A TYPICAL DAY

"I have worked both morning and afternoon shifts on Sundays. This is what a typical, two-shift day is like. For the morning shift, I normally arrive at the aquarium at 8:00 A.M. and sign in at the volunteer office. After that I report to the curator of birds to see if there will be any changes in my schedule that day. For example, if there's been a birth of a new penguin, or the death of a bird, my duties for the day might be altered.

"I then prepare the food for all the free-flying birds in the Amazon exhibit, including the red-capped cardinals, aracari, boat-billed herons, conures, and Amazon parrots. Their diet consists of chopped fruits, nuts, and mealworms. I take their food up to the feeding trays in the exhibit and refill all the seed bowls and water bowls. At approximately 8:30 A.M. we take the macaws that are scheduled to be perched that day out of their cages and down to their perches. I then return upstairs and give fresh food and seeds to all the parrots and macaws that are not to be perched that day. I also remove all the dishes from the macaw cages so they can be cleaned and their new diets for that day can be prepared.

"At 10:30 A.M. I clean and prepare the fish and assemble the vitamin supplements for the penguin feeding show at 11:00 A.M. From 11:00 to 11:30 A.M. we feed the penguins and record their eating habits. If there are babies in the exhibit, they are weighed, and if there are nesting penguins, they are fed on the nest. I return to food prep and clean the fish bucket.

"I then have a break until about 1:00 P.M. During my break, though, I often bathe, exercise, and treat the birds, as well as have my own lunch.

"During the afternoon shift we generally hold a question-and-answer period with visitors to the exhibit. At around 2:00 P.M. I return to the cage area and clean cages, fill all the seed bowls and water bowls, and clean the surrounding area. The cleaning generally takes approximately one hour, and I then head to food prep to prepare the macaw fruit diets and the fish for the penguin's second feeding show.

"At 4:00 P.M. we do another penguin feeding show. At the close of this second show, the staff member remains behind to clean the exhibit, and I head to food prep to clean the bucket and tally the penguin feeding chart, which helps the curator determine if penguins are pregnant or about to molt. Then I take the macaw diets to the third floor and prepare the cages for the birds to be brought back to them. I pick up all the bowls from the free-flying bird diets that I put out at 8:00 A.M. At 4:30 P.M. the macaws are brought back up to their cages and all the doors are secured. I leave the aquarium by 5:00 P.M."

THE UPSIDES AND DOWNSIDES

"I love working with the birds and getting to meet people from all over. I've been teaching the birds tricks and learning about all the different positions that are available in the aquarium.

"The obvious drawbacks are getting bitten, having to clean cages, and smelling like fish when you go home. Another drawback for the actual staff members is the low pay."

A WORD OF ADVICE

"As a volunteer, you obviously would need to have a real job. As for someone looking to go into this as a profession, I would recommend they also consider having another job. The pay is very low for a starting aquarist, and it isn't much better for those in higher positions. You have to really love what you are doing. You take a lot of abuse from the public and from the animals."

Mary Hooper, Volunteer

Mary Hooper plays three roles. She is a part-time college student, a volunteer at the Phoenix Zoo, and a paid worker there as well. Currently, Mary is attending Phoenix College with plans to transfer to Arizona State University. "I am planning for a degree in zoology," Mary explains, "a long and winding road, and with that, I don't know where I'll go. Honestly, I want to take over for Siegfried and Roy in Las Vegas, but they don't know that yet!

"My passion is for cats, so maybe I'll pursue something with the government, working on conservation and wildlife projects or as a trainer and educator. My short-term goal is to be a keeper at a zoo for experience and knowledge. My long-term goal? Not at a zoo! Zoo's are great for their breeding programs and education programs, but I don't want to send my message through a zoo. It is really important to me to help people experience the wonders of nature, and if I can help preserve a fraction of it, I'll be happy."

MARY HOOPER'S PAID POSITION

Mary works as a birthday party coordinator in the PR department at the Phoenix Zoo in Arizona. She started working there in 1995 as a custodian, and she has been the birthday party coordinator since November of 1996.

"I hope to become an animal keeper within the next few years," Mary says, "but for now, I have my foot in the door. I work Monday, Wednesday, Friday, Saturday, and Sunday. On the weekdays I am in an office returning phone calls, answering questions about birthday parties at the zoo, and scheduling parties. I handle all of the paperwork and money involved. I make an order once a week for supplies for the parties, and I also take an end-of-month inventory.

"On Saturday and Sunday I host the birthday parties in the specific party area. There are time slots for four parties a day on each weekend day.

"I like the environment I work in the best. The zoo is a wonderful place to work as well as learn about the natural world. The thing I don't like is seeing people at the zoo who don't clean up after themselves and don't seem to appreciate the natural world.

"The zoo has much to offer to the public besides animals. We have people to do just about everything here! Since the zoo is not a government zoo, we try many things to get funds to operate. We offer activities such as summer camp, night camp, birthday parties and special events, weddings or picnics, for example.

"I handle everything that has to do with birthday parties. Many children love the zoo and jump at the chance to have their birthday parties there. The parties are held at a special ramada. At the ramada there are three exhibits in view, as well as a lake with many birds to watch. I like to educate the children and tell them what I know about the surrounding area and the zoo."

MARY HOOPER'S VOLUNTEER POSITION

"I have volunteered at the zoo since September of 1995. I probably wouldn't have even thought of volunteering if I hadn't worked there already! I started as a volunteer keeper aide. I had to complete certain animal handling classes to qualify. Once I finished the classes, I began to volunteer.

"My duties as a keeper aide included general cleaning and feeding of the Education Department animals. These are animals that are used for education in the form of animal presentations, both on the grounds at the zoo and off grounds at schools and certain events. I helped the keeper with cleaning specific areas and preparing food and distributing food.

"That program was expanded and a new program began, which included all participating keepers throughout the whole zoo. The new program is called VAC (volunteer animal caregiver). I couldn't do both, so I became a VAC with more training and a test to qualify.

"In the first program I volunteered about sixteen hours a month, and with the new program, I volunteer about eight to twelve hours a month.

"In addition to the on-grounds volunteering that I do, I am also part of a zoo volunteer group called the AOT (animal observation team). The AOT participates in many activities. The one I am involved with goes mountain lion tracking four times a year. We work with a biologist who works with ranchers to determine how many cats are located in certain areas. And, of course, there are requirements to be met to participate, such as workshops and a test.

"I hope this volunteer experience and my job at the zoo in addition to my education will help me to reach my long-term goals."

A WORD OF ADVICE

"I do think it's important for people to know that everyone working at zoos doesn't necessarily start off in his or her desired area. I was a custodian much longer than I have been the birthday party coordinator. Start at the bottom if you have to. It's a great way to learn all aspects of a working facility."

PROFESSIONAL ASSOCIATIONS

The following list of associations can be used as a valuable resource guide in locating additional information about specific careers. Many of the organizations publish newsletters listing job and internship opportunities, and still others offer an employment service to members. A quick look at the organizations' names will give you an idea of the scope of zoo work.

ZOO AND AQUARIUM ASSOCIATIONS

Zoo associations have been formed in many different countries. The largest is the American Association of Zoological Parks and Aquariums, founded in 1924. Other zoo federations include those of Great Britain and Ireland, Spain and Spanish America, Japan, Poland, and Germany. Related organizations include the International Union of Directors of Zoological Gardens and the Wild Animal Propagation Trust. These organizations disseminate information on zoo management, exchange of specimens, and conservation of wildlife.

American Association of Zoological Parks and Aquariums
   7970-D Old Georgetown Road
   Bethesda, MD 20114

American Zoo and Aquarium Association
    Executive Office and Conservation Center
    7970-D Old Georgetown Road
    Bethesda, MD 20814-2493

American Zoo and Aquarium Association
    Office of Membership Services
    Oglebay Park
    Wheeling, WV 26003-1698

ANIMAL CARETAKING

For information on animal caretaking and the animal shelter and control personnel training program, write to:

American Association of Zookeepers
    635 SW Gage Boulevard
    Topeka, KS 66606

Animal Caretakers Information
    The Humane Society of the United States
    Companion Animals Division, Suite 100
    5430 Grosvenor Lane
    Bethesda, MD 20814

To obtain a list of grooming schools or the name of the nearest certified dog groomer in your area, send a stamped self-addressed envelope to:

National Dog Groomers Association of America
    Box 101
    Clark, PA 16113

For information on training and certification of kennel staff and owners, contact:

American Boarding Kennel Association
    4575 Galley Road, Suite 400-A
    Colorado Springs, CO 80915

ANIMAL BEHAVIOR

Animal School, Inc.
Dr. Mary Nitschke
Koll Business Center, Building 9
7850 SW Nimbus Avenue
Beaverton, OR 97005

EATM (Exotic Animal Training and Management)
7075 Campus Road
Moorpark, CA 93021
(A two-year training program)

Association for the Study of Animal Behaviour
The Membership Secretary
82A High Street
Sawston Cambridge
England CB2 4HJ

IMATA (International Marine Animal Trainers Association)
1720 South Shores Road
San Diego, CA 92109
This organization can provide you with a list of recognized training programs.

Latham Foundation
"Promoting respect for all life through education."
Latham Plaza Building
Clement and Schillers Streets
Alameda, CA 94501

VETERINARY MEDICINE AND VETERINARY TECHNOLOGY ASSOCIATIONS

For information on careers in veterinary medicine and veterinary technology contact:

American Association of Zoo Veterinarians
Dr. Wilbur Amand, Executive Director
6 North Pennell Road
Media, PA 19063

American Veterinary Medical Association
1931 North Meacham Road, Suite 100
Schaumburg, IL 60173-4360

For information on veterinary education contact:

Association of American Veterinary Medical Colleges
1101 Vermont Avenue NW, Suite 710
Washington, DC 20005

For information on scholarships, grants, and loans, contact the financial aid office at the veterinary schools to which you wish to apply.

VOLUNTEERING

If you are interested in becoming a volunteer, contact your local zoo or aquarium. Information on docent activities is also available from:

Association of Zoo and Aquarium Docents
9507 Roe Avenue
Overland Park, KS 66207

WILDLIFE REHABILITATION

The National Wildlife Rehabilitators Association is an organization for people interested and concerned about the welfare of wildlife. Structured mainly for active rehabilitators, NWRA membership also includes professional wildlife personnel, conservationists, educators, naturalists, researchers, veterinarians, people from zoos and humane societies, and many others interested in improving knowledge of wild animals and in assuring their survival. The NWRA is incorporated solely for the support of the science and profession of wildlife rehabilitation and its practitioners.

For more information and to become a member contact:

National Wildlife Rehabilitators Association
    Central Office
    14 North Seventh Avenue
    St. Cloud, MN 56303

The International Wildlife Rehabilitation Council (IWRC) is a professional organization for wildlife rehabilitators, founded to develop and disseminate information on the rehabilitation and care of wild animals, with the goal of returning them to their native environment.

For more information and to become a member, contact:

International Wildlife Rehabilitation Council
    4437 Central Place, Suite B-4
    Suisun City, CA 94585

WILDLIFE REHABILITATION PUBLICATIONS

AZA CONSERVATION AND SCIENCE PUBLICATIONS AND REPORTS

The following two publications are available from:

American Association of Zoological Parks and Aquariums
7970-D Old Georgetown Road
Bethesda, MD 20114

Species Survival Plans: Strategies for Wildlife Conservation. AZA Annual Report on Conservation and Science.

Conservation Resource Guide. Various technical and popular articles, fact sheets, brochures, and directory updates.

OTHER PUBLICATIONS

Basic Wildlife Rehabilitation 1AB, by Jan White, DVM. This is the manual that goes along with the Basic Wildlife Rehabilitation 1AB skills seminar; upon completion of the seminar you are "certified." Includes medical and diet calculation information.

International Wildlife Rehabilitation Council
    4437 Central Place, Suite B-4
    Suisun, CA 94585

Care and Rehabilitation of Injured Owls, fourth ed. by Katherine McKeever. An excellent resource book for anyone who deals with raptors of any kind.

W. F. Rannie
    P. O. Box 700
    Beamsville, Ontario, L0R 1B0
    Canada

Caring for Birds of Prey, by Jerry Olsen.

Faculty of Education
    University of Canberra
    P.O. Box 1
    Belconnen ACT
    Australia 2615

The *Center for Wildlife Law* quarterly newsletter. For a complimentary copy write to:

Center for Wildlife Law
    1117 Stanford NE
    Albuquerque, NM 87131

The Exotic Animal Formulary, by Dr. James W. Carpenter.

Veterinary Specialty Products, Inc.
    P.O. Box 812005
    Boca Raton, FL 33481

Housing Avian Insectivores During Rehabilitation, by Paul D. and Georgean Z. Kyle.

Driftwood Wildlife Association
    P.O. Box 39
    Driftwood, TX 78619

Living With Wildlife, a Sierra Club book by the California Center for Wildlife with Diana Landau and Shelley Stump. A good book for the general public; stresses who is qualified to care for injured and orphaned animals and also gives information on rehabilitation, permits, etc. It's available in most bookstores.

Primer of Wildlife Care & Rehabilitation, by Patti L. Raley. Contains extensive diet information, lab techniques, veterinary information, zoonoses, charts with species information, etc.

Brukner Nature Center
  5995 Horseshoe Bend Road
  Troy, OH 45373

Raptor Rehabilitation—A Manual of Guidelines, by the Carolina Raptor Center.

Carolina Raptor Center (Mathias Engelmann and Pat Marcum)
  P.O. Box 16443
  Charlotte, NC 28297-6443

The Songbird Diet Index, by Marcy Rule.

Coconut Creek Publishing Company
  2201 NW Terrace
  Coconut Creek, FL 33066-2032

State Wildlife Laws Handbook, by Ruth S. Musgrave and Maryann Stein.

The University of New Mexico Center for Wildlife Law
  4 Research Place, Suite 200
  Rockville, MD 20850

Training Opportunities for Rehabilitators, NWRA. A list of all the locations available in the United States for internship opportunities in wildlife rehabilitation.

NWRA Publications
    14 North Seventh Avenue
    St. Cloud, MN 56303

Wild Animal Care and Rehabilitation Manual, fourth ed., by the
    Kalamazoo Nature Center.

Kalamazoo Nature Center
    7000 North Westnedge Avenue
    Kalamazoo, MI 49007

Wildlife Feeding and Nutrition, by Charles T. Robbins, Academic
    Press.

Wildlife Rehabilitation and Care Manual, by Wildlife Welfare,
    Inc.

Wildlife Welfare, Inc.
    c/o Jan Eisenhower Jackson
    4216 Mountainbrook Road
    Apex, NC 2750

*Wildlife Rehabilitation Minimum Standards & Accreditation
    Program,* by IWRC and NWRA (recommended for all wildlife
    rehabilitators).

IWRC
    4437 Central Place, Suite B-4
    Suisun, CA 94585

Wild Ones (sell a variety of books on wildlife rehabilitation and
    others, and can order in anything you request).

Wild Ones
    P.O. Box 947
    Springville, CA 93265-0947

Wildlife Rehabilitation Today, published quarterly by:

Coconut Creek Publishing Company
    2201 NW Fortieth Terrace
    Coconut Creek, FL 33066-2032

Willowbrook Wildlife Haven Volunteer Handbook by Willowbrook
  Wildlife Haven. An excellent volunteer manual. Good for
  general information as well as a model for volunteer manuals.
  Good species care and natural history information.

Willowbrook Wildlife Haven
  P.O. Box 2339
  Glen Ellyn, IL 60138

  Single copies of the following publications on wildlife rehabilitation are available at publication cost from:

Human Dimensions Research Unit
  Department of Natural Resources
  Fernow Hall
  Cornell University
  Ithaca, NY 14853

American Wildlife & Plants (a guide to wildlife food habits)

Raptor Biomedicine

Raptor Rehabilitation (a manual of guidelines offered by the Carolina
  Raptor Center)

The Songbird Diet Index

State Wildlife Laws Handbook

Training Opportunities for Rehabilitators

Wild Animal Care and Rehabilitation Manual

Wildlife Feeding and Nutrition

Wildlife Rehabilitation and Care Manual

Wildlife Rehabilitation Minimum Standards & Accreditation Program

Willowbrook Wildlife Center's Pharmaceutical Index

Willowbrook Wildlife Haven Volunteer Handbook

ADDITIONAL RESOURCES

Many other rehabilitation books and handouts are available through the NWRA and IWRC.

National Wildlife Rehabilitators Association (NWRA)
  NWRA Office
  14 North Seventh Avenue
  St. Cloud, MN 56303

International Wildlife Rehabilitation Council (IWRC)
  4437 Central Place, Suite B-4
  Suisun, CA 94585

CONTACTS FOR STATE AND FEDERAL REHABILITATION PERMITS

For a state rehabilitation license, contact the Department of Wildlife Resources, located in the phone book in each state capital.

For a federal permit, contact the regional office closest to where you live.

U.S. FISH & WILDLIFE SERVICE REGIONAL OFFICES

Region One

California, Hawaii, Idaho, Nevada, Oregon, Washington, and Pacific Territories

U.S. Fish & Wildlife Service
Office of Migratory Bird Permits
911 N.E. Eleventh Avenue
Portland, OR 97232-4181

Region Two

Arizona, New Mexico, Oklahoma, and Texas

U.S. Fish & Wildlife Service
Migratory Bird Office/Permits
P.O. Box 709
Albuquerque, NM 87103-0709

Region Three

Illinois, Indiana, Iowa, Michigan, Minnesota, Missouri, Ohio, and Wisconsin

Applications Examiner, Law Enforcement
  United States Department of the Interior
  Fish and Wildlife Service
  P.O. Box 45
  Federal Building, Fort Snelling
  St. Paul, MN 55111

Region Four

Alabama, Arkansas, Florida, Georgia, Kentucky, Louisiana, Mississippi, North Carolina, South Carolina, Tennessee, Puerto Rico, and U.S. Virgin Islands

Richard B. Russell Federal Building
  75 Spring Street SW, Suite 1276
  Atlanta, GA 30303

Region Five

Connecticut, Delaware, District of Columbia, Maine, Maryland, Massachusetts, New Hampshire, New Jersey, New York, Pennsylvania, Rhode Island, Vermont, Virginia, and West Virginia

Assistant Regional Director (LE)
  U.S. Fish & Wildlife Service
  P.O. Box 779
  Hadley, MA 01035

Region Six

Colorado, Kansas, Montana, Nebraska, North Dakota, South Dakota, Utah, and Wyoming

Denver Federal Center
    Box 25486
    Denver, CO 80225

Region Seven

Alaska

U.S. Fish & Wildlife Service
    Division of Law Enforcement
    P.O. Box 92597
    Anchorage, AK 99509-2597

ADDRESSES OF
FEATURED INSTITUTIONS

Animal School, Inc.
  Dr. Mary Nitschke
  Koll Business Center, Building 9
  7850 SW Nimbus Avenue
  Beaverton, OR 97005

Aquarium of the Americas
  One Canal Street
  New Orleans, LA 70130

Audubon Zoological Garden
  6500 Magazine Street
  New Orleans, LA 70130

Austin Zoo
  Rawhide Trail
  P.O. Box 91808
  Austin, TX 78709-1808

Detroit Zoological Institute
  West Ten Mile Road and Woodward Avenue
  P.O. Box 39
  Royal Oak, MI 48068-0039

La Guardar Inc. Wildlife and Rehabilitation Center
  4966 Country Road 656
  Webster, FL 33597

Lion Country Safari
    2003 Lion Country Safari Road
    Loxahatchee, FL 33470

Los Angeles Zoo
    5333 Zoo Drive
    Los Angeles, CA 90027-1498

Metro Washington Park Zoo
    4001 SW Canyon Road
    Portland, OR 97221

Miami Metrozoo
    12400 SW 152nd Street
    Miami, FL 33177

New England Aquarium
    Central Wharf
    Boston, MA 02110-3399

Phoenix Zoo
    455 North Galvin Parkway
    Phoenix, AZ 85008